Published by

ATLANTIC

PUBLISHERS & DISTRIBUTORS (P) LTD

7/22, Ansari Road, Darya Ganj, New Delhi-110002
Phones : +91-11-40775252, 40775214, 23273880, 23275880
Fax: +91-11-23285873
Web: www.atlanticbooks.com
E-mail: orders@atlanticbooks.com

Printed & bound in India by Atlantic Print Services

Preface

The idea of this enquiry into Shaw's idea of the superman was introduced and nurtured during my post-graduate studies at Magadh University, Bodh Gaya, by the inspiring and loving guidance of my teacher, Dr. J. P. Singh, to whom I owe a debt of gratitude far too deep for words.

I am proud to acknowledge my reverence and gratefulness for my supervisor, Dr. J. S. Shaw (Pro-Vice-Chancellor, Bhagalpur University) whose patience with me and indulgence in my toil, made it possible for me to complete my work.

Dr. V. N. Mishra, University Professor of English, Bhagalpur University (at present Director, Adult and Continuing Education), gave me the guidance and affection of a guardian, providing inspiration and caution at every turn,—for which gratitude is a far too formal word.

Devendra Kumar Singh

Contents

	Preface	*iii*
I.	Introduction: The Seed	1
II.	The Sapling	18
III.	The Tree	42
IV.	The Flowers and the Fruits	62
V.	The Shadow	72
	Select Bibliography	86

I

Introduction: The Seed

I

In preparing this book I have been guided by a natural inclination to understand G.B. Shaw's concept of Superman. Plato's 'new man' is the basic and fundamental concept of the *Republic*. Plato desired to make an evolution of man into new man in his *Republic* by the process of selection of breeding. He regarded marriage as a legal prostitution and advanced his convincing argument willingly to weed out the system of marriage. Plato's concept of superman is limited to this plan; while Shaw envisages a higher level of understanding reached not by jumping over the earlier stages. In other words, while Plato's doctrine of new man has been emotional and sometimes even sentimental, Shaw has sought an intellectual projection of ideas based on highly convincing facts and figures. This superman does not represent a fall or waste of goodness but reveals the cosmic rhythm of life through which he achieves perfection in his thought. Plato desired to root out the system of marriage without going into the ethics and romance of this rite. It is a fact that society has outgrown marriage system but has made no modification in the institution of marriage and here lies the profundity of Shaw.

The development of Shaw's concept of superman may be examined in the form of a growing image which in the beginning is in the shape of seed growing into sapling tree, flower and fruit. The Greek attitude finds a substantive expression in Plato's book *The Republic* which is marked by a well-calculated vision and design. There is no doubt, a core of conflict and comedy in this view, but in the final resolution it represents the cosmic rhythm of life. By cosmic rhythm, I have meant the movement of life through growth, maturity and decay to resurrection. The cosmic rhythm of life embodies the process of creative evolution, maturity

maturity through evolutionary man into superman. This I have taken to be the essence of the 'cosmic' both Greek and Shavian. Shaw's theory of *Life-force* helps to a great extent in the emergence of superman.

Plato's selection of breeding bears a close resemblance to Shaw's ideas but after all there is a difference in the degree of thought and process. Plato's accent on rooting out the system of marriage is neither a creative approach nor conducive to the evolution of man into superman. The system in itself is an art and it does not simply beautify the thought and norms of life but also cooperates in bringing a true harmony between a male and a female. The system is also a cause and condition of the evolution of man into superman.

In the first Chapter of the book I have made an attempt to understand George Bernard Shaw as a thinker who exercised an eclectic passion for ideas to shape his own thought. The birth of superman is not an accident but is the result of a creative and gradual evolutionary process. Shaw's hatred for his father's drunkenness and his love for his mother, shows his outright thought and attitude to sexual relationship. In his experience and thinking about sex, the aim is to understand the significance of love as a biological principle involving the evolution of man into superman. Like marriage, it is the first and foremost condition for procreation and breeding. This biological basis is essential to marriage because this is what constitutes and beautifies the institution of marriage. Evolution is never an accident but a creative and gradual process. His doctrine of superman bears a close stamp of similarity with that of Nietzsche. But after all there is a difference between George Bernard Shaw and Nietzsche. Nietzsche's Superman is an outcome of biological and evolutionary factors to which Shaw adds the environmental factors such as society, economics, politics, education and family.

In the first Chapter of the book I have chiefly focused my attention on the process of formation of the seed of superman in Shaw. The impact of Bergson, Plato, Nietzsche and a number of philosophers made a clear impact on Shaw and it helped in a great way in shaping his idea of superman. Shaw's superman does not seem to me a solution of the problem of modern life. Shaw is obsessed with the causes of delay of evolution of man into superman in most of his plays. In *Candida*, he craves for the socialism of right between a husband and a wife. Candida is no longer a ghost or a windbag of morality like her husband and thus

Shaw seems to be roaring very soundly and convincingly to bridge up the gap between a husband and a wife Shaw's sympathy, just like John Galsworthy's, goes to the female and the downtrodden. It is obvious in *Candida* that Shaw puts the blame on the society which creates barriers in the evolution of superman. He even exposes the weaknesses of the romantic fervour because it distracts from the gradual evolution of man into superman. He hates romance as he hates beef.

Shaw appears to be a champion of the causes of human problems. He seems to have caught the knack of delving deep into the problems of human life. He seems to have adopted the weapon of non-violence for achieving the mission of his life like M.K. Gandhi. It is a fact that he is revolutionary only in theory and not in practice. When Gandhi was shot dead by Nathuram Godse, he said that to be too good is dangerous. The mission of his life was to bring a radical change in the social-economic condition of human life. His theory of *Life-Force* is an addition to and an improvement upon his doctrine of creative evolution. Unlike D.H. Lawrence, Shaw does not retain his trust in the theory of *Blood-mysticism*. His theory of *Life-Force* is not a negation of will-power but an improvement upon it. He hammers on the theory of *Life-Force* as the cause and condition of the flow of human life.

Shaw has made a naked demonstration of his hatred for the institution of marriage because in his opinion the present system of marriage does not suit the needs of evolution. It is a plain truth that marriage is one of the greatest blocks in the procreation of superman for Shaw. Marriage is not a social contract between a male and a female but on the other hand it is a kind of harmonious adjustment between a male and a female. He exhibits the importance of intellect which is also a noteworthy factor in the development of human race. In his period of profound thinking which coincided with the period of his great thought-provoking comedies, Shaw expatiated on the theory of *Life-Force* operating through the association of an intellectual male and female combined together in an idyllic socialism. Disparity is a hindrance in the process of evolution of man into superman.

Shaw in his theory of *Life-Force* gave man the second place in relation to woman in the context of evolution of man into superman. Man becomes an agent in the grip of *Life-Force* whose immediate channel is woman. Candida, like other heroines of the plays, yields to

Morell because the preserving instinct of *Life-Force* can be satiated in the sheltering figure of Morell. She is not only an embodiment of reason and Christian attributes but also an exponent of the theory of *Life-Force*. The theories of *Life-Force*, creative evolution, and will-power are central to his great masterpieces. Raina's love for Bluntschli marks the perfection of Shaw's thought of creative evolution. She does not yield to Sergius because Life-Force will be frustrated by lack of protective guarantees that Bluntschli has. Similarly had Candida surrendered to Marchbank, the very purpose of Shaw's thought might have been aborted. The credit goes to Shaw for backing philosophy into drama. *Caesar and Cleopatra* marks the turning tide of Bernard Shaw's fortune and fame. Truly speaking the true qualities of a modern play are that it should play and that it should pay. Shakespeare wrote *Antony and Cleopatra* and *Julius Caesar*. What really annoys Shaw about Shakespeare that he sees quite as clearly like Shaw that Brutus is unpractical and ineffectual; but he also sees what is quite as plain and practical. *Julius Caesar* seems to be only an endeavour in tragic art – a kind of first phase in the process. Shakespeare, unlike Shaw, sees the tragic principle operating in human life not only through resistance from the other impulse but also through the impact of evil, through the limitations of human world as well as through extraordinary intensity of feeling and thought and imagination: Hamlet with his highly speculative mind, Othello with his elementary nature and Antony with his grand sweeping passion of love.

The second Chapter of the book closely examines the development of the idea of the superman through *Man and Superman*, *Mrs. Warren's Profession* and *Back to Methuselah*. Shaw seems to have received a serious impact of Nietzsche but he never follows the theory of Nietzsche blindly. The birth of superman is the fundamental demand at all times. Shaw's superman is not a product of some extraordinary external force but on the other hand he is the outcome of the interplay of different factors, like selection of sex, theory of creative evolution etc. His superman, unlike Plato's, is a creature of blood and flesh. *Man and Superman* makes an exposition of his exciting ideas. The *Life-Force* acts primarily through woman who involves a man for the sole purpose of procreation. Man becomes a feeble agent in the grip of life-force. The life-force acts as a selecting agent and puts better men and women together. It is not easily seen that the trampling of the ideals even by casual supermen like a Caesar or a Napoleon is a preparation for what is to come. In Back to

Methuselah written about twenty years later, he makes an addition of another concept, the concept of creative evolution, Life-force is at the root of all creation while creative evolution is the cause of every growth that occurs in a living organism. The desire for change for the better emerges in the mind of Adam and it is one of the motivating forces behind creative evolution. When the desire for a change for the better grips the mind, life-force merges into creative evolution. The desire for change stirs the imagination operating as an agent of creative evolution, creates and evolves the species. Shaw's theory of life-force and his doctrine of creative evolution can operate well only in the political, social, economic, individual equality of human beings and the sexes. Shaw differs basically from Plato in the process of creation of Superman. Plato's superman is a deformed creature. The evolution of superman in the view of shaw depends chiefly on the biological factor.

I have presented Shaw's hatred for marriage in the play *Heart Break House, Getting Married* and *Mrs. Warren's Profession*. Shaw strongly pleads for abrogation of the institution of marriage in *Getting Married* because it is not conducive for the birth of Superman. He insists upon the idea that marriage is no longer a permanent certificate of a permanent love between a husband and a wife. His trust in Christianity seems to have been lost in *Man and Superman*. But it is restored with modifications in *Back to Methuselah*. In *Mrs. Warren's Profession* he strongly insists on the value of education which helps to a great extent in shaping a child's destiny and his evolution into a superman. Mrs. Warren offers a healthy education to Miss Vivie by engaging herself in the dirty game of prostitution.

The sacrifice of Mrs. Warren demonstrates an advanced idea of Shaw. She is like a flower born to blush unseen. She sacrifices her pleasure for giving a better shape to the destiny of Miss Vivie. Mrs. Warren is not a born harlot but she was made a harlot by the choice forced on her by society. The socio-economic condition has turned her life in the life of queen. Had she been born in a rich family, she could have been as great as Napoleon or Caesar or St. Joan. Unfortunately she had to sell her body for the gratification of her life-long cherished desire. She desired to see Miss Vivie not compelled to live like a prostitute but like a gentle woman. She finds a greater satisfaction to learn that her child has made a stupendous progress. Thus we see that evolution of man into superman is not an external process but an internal creative gradual process.

In the third Chapter of the book, I have mainly presented Shaw's concept of Superman which is re-enforced in his *Back to Methuselah.* His theory of *Life-Force* is neither mystified nor overshadowed by his obsession with sex. Ann in *Man and Superman* appears to be chasing Tanner and it shows that man is the game and female is the hunter. Shaw is confirmed that the birth of superman requires an improvement of wisdom and morality. The idea of 'wisdom' seems to have been borrowed from Plato's *The Republic.* Plato symbolises grades of wisdom in gold, silver and iron. Wisdom is one of the ruling force behind the creation of superman. Shaw describes his *Back to Methuselah* as another legend of creative evolution. This metabiological pentateuch is not only a resurrection of the thought of the earlier work but also a major and drastic improvement of it. His lost trust in Christianity finds a glorious resurrection in his *Back to Methuselah.* Adam knows well that he is the child of immortality. It appears that Shaw is very close to Wordsworth's Plantonism in his doctrine of immortality. He generated another theory which may be called the theory of *will-power.* Will-power has a greater role in the evolution of man into superman. It is not simply a necessity of evolution of man into superman but also a basic and fundamental requisition of life. No doubt, imagination is the faculty of creation. We create what we desire. Shaw's dynamic philosophy comes to its fulfilment in *Back to Methuselah.* His new religion as evident in this great masterpiece is a metaphysical trust in a metaphysical life-force, of whose spiritual evolution is the outcome.

His theory of creative evolution is Lamarckian and Butlerian. It is Butlerian in the sense that living organisms get changed due to their strong inner desire to change. Shaw is greatly obliged to Butler who was the greatest writer of the later half of the 19th Century in his own *circle.* Shaw and Butler seem to depend on a common trust that effort and will are two ruling conditions of evolution. Shaw gives a great importance to women in the hard competition of evolution because she is the cause and condition of both creation and evolution.

The fourth Chapter of the book exhibits Shaw's satirical vein and anger against the kind of people presented in *Back to Methuselah.* Shaw has presented a dismal picture inhabited by superwomen and supermen in his *Back to Methuselah.* The note of agony and hope for a change for the better at which the play ends is a kind of epilogue which the writer of *Man and Superman* could not perceive. The playwright who took down the last scene of *Back to Methuselah* is, virtually, not the man who wrote *Man and Superman*. The vision remains the same but the spirit has changed. The distance between the two great plays is no less great than the distance between the *Comedy of Errors* and *The Tempest*. Shaw seems to be smiling sweetly at the kind of people who hardly have any sense of value and worth apart from the pleasure of human life. The love for art and lust for sex do not hold any distinctive meaning to them. They are taxed with their lives. One gets a slight note of humour in learning that the supermen and superwomen are born of eggs. At the age of four they get matured and it becomes a laughing stock to the readers. Shaw has created not an ideal race for the common people but on the other hand he has foreshadowed a world of Utopia. All that makes life pleasant art, literature, music, dance, fancy, love and painting—has scarcely any meaning for the young people of this Utopia. Does it not bear a close resemblance with the kind of race that Jonathan Swift presents in his *Gulliver's Travels*? The incident of slaughtering of Pygmalion and of the two dolls created by him is a figurative representation of the murder of creative potentiality of every kind. It is a bit rather absurd and ridiculous to trust that Swift could consider horses to be the idea race who had the right to rule over mankind. In the case of Bernard Shaw, one is bound to be tempted to trust that the artist was creating a race of ideal people with his tongue in the cheek.

The supermen and superwomen as they figure in *Back to Methuselah* are not alone the ugliest people imaginable but also shoddily dressed. The She-Ancient is equal to the Ancient without any lust for sex. Her sex is perceivable only by her voice because her breasts appear to be manly. The elders of the world of the superman are neither happy nor their destiny is bright. The modern people are taxed with their liabilities which keep them struggling tor their identity throughout their lives. But it hardly matters to the superpersons of *Back to Methuselah*.

The people of the 20th Century are not disgusted with the problems of their lives and body, in the way in which superpersons of Shaw's Utopia are. The diseases, the murders, the day-to-day persecution and a number of other problems hardly stir the modern man as the superpersons of Shaw's Utopia find themselves to be. Even one of the organic characters of the play is equally sobbing, sighing and writing with grief by what has taken place. She knew love and nourished her children in her womb. But new love, the great sustainer of life is dead, and all that remains is a life of eternity devoid of all passion, emotion. Lilith makes a brutal attack on the civilisation of these people. No doubt man has bagged success acquiring super human strength but has lost the vital power which made life worthwhile. It is a fact that Shaw, like a great artist and a great well-wisher of the people, is laughing at the kind of superpersons as figuring in *Back to Methuselah*. Thus it is clear, what the superman of part V of *Back to Methuselah* has achieved is not something that George Bernard Shaw considered to be ideal for mankind. It is aberration rather than evolution. The world of Utopia in reality is a world of deformed creatures and Shaw strongly desired mankind to avert an evolution in that direction.

II

Philosophy is said to be an attempt to explain the mystery of life and universe. In other words, philosophy is an attempt to know what really exists and what merely appears to be. Some of the philosophers hold the opinion that philosophy is an intellectual explanation of human experience as a whole. Flint defines philosophy as "the highest thought about the highest thing."[1] If this definition of philosophy is accepted, G.B. Shaw cannot claim a place in the rank of "Philosophers". But the fact remains that Shaw has taken up, in some of the most important of his plays, a problem which rises above social or historical confines and acquires a universal significance. It is the problem of the evolution of man into superman and of the adjustment of this new race to the life of the Utopian community which may emerge thereafter. Even if such a vision does not deserve to be called a "high thought", Shaw cannot be denied a place with thinkers like Plato and Nietzsche.

The Personality of George Bernard Shaw was unique. He had neither the pleasure of respect nor money to pay for pleasure. His egoism led him to seek for intellectual pastures where he could support his mighty brain and thereby excel in the only field that was open to him. His intellectual pursuits convinced him that he was born to do greater things than running after pleasure. He said once "I was born to educate England."[2] He was the voice of his age just as Dr. Johnson was the voice of his age. He crusaded against the smug beliefs of his time and fought for ideas many of

1. Joseph Gerald Brennan, *The Meaning of Philosophy*, and Row Publishers, New York, Evenston and London, 1953, p. 2.
2. Quoted by H.C. Duffin: *The Quintessence of Bernard Shaw*, General Book Depot, Delhi, 1939, p. 17.

which were unacceptable to his contemporaries. He has been described by some critics as an anesthema to the smug world of respectability.

Shaw's dominating personality made people to accept his logically sound ideas as philosophy. His rationality, strictly speaking, was the product of his disturbing intellect. He had a passion for tackling the problems of humanity. He tempered with ideas in the same way in which Socrates had done in his time. He, however, did not take hemlock like Keats to drink but laurels to pride upon. Rationality with him was not a theoretical device but a fully practical tool. He believed in the power of ideas because ideas can influence man's action. Even the concept of superman is not the product of inspiration but is based on reason.

Early in his youth Shaw took upon himself the task of changing the world, and since he had not learnt by then the art of wielding the pen, he took recourse to oratory. He was an acknowledged public speaker before he was a dramatist. As an orator, he was very effective. Mr. Joad thinks that "he never heard him making bad speech. The effectiveness of his oratory was due to the magic of his voice which vibrated through the melodies of intonation and articulation. Shaw was never dull; he was amusing, brilliant, often startling, partly because of his gift for apt smile."[1]

As a critic of contemporary society, Shaw was merciless both in his speeches and writings. But he was at heart a very kind person who could not tolerate physical harm done to anybody. He was as solicitious of the welfare of birds and beasts as he was to men and women. But he never made an exhibition of his tenderness of heart; as a matter of fact, he tried to hide it from others. G.K. Chesterton writes:

> He would defy any laws or lose any friends to show mercy to the humblest beast or the most kidden bird; yet I cannot recall in the whole of his works or in the whole of his conversation a single word of tenderness or beast.[2]

He further says:

> Of the many sincere things Mr. Shaw has said a more sincere one than when he stated he was a vegetarian not because of his eating meat was bad morality but because it was of bad taste.[5]

1. R.N. Roy: *Benard Shaw's Philosophy of Life*, F.A. K.L. Mukhopadhyay, Calcutta, 1964, p. 10.
2. *Ibid.*, p. 41.

D.H. Lawrence considers an intuitive approach to life much more powerful and desirable than the intellectual approach. Intellect has got to be transcended by an artist. But Shaw is not interested in art's hedonistic perspective but art as a vehicle for the expression of ideas. He looks at the world with pensive eyes and with magnifying glasses and is shocked at the state of things. He grunts and grumbles in a guardian's spirit of anger and hammers home his point with his power of intelligence. New ideas swarm his fertile mind and he has something new to say on love, religion, prostitution, government, the superman, monarchy, democracy, crime, liberty, slavery, charity, economy, women, empire and everything else that he happens to talk about. The inadequacy of the institution of marriage troubles him much. He appears not in the guise of a jestler but of a philosopher, not of the mount-bank but of the prophet. Sometimes the method is certainly that of a jester but not the matter. He talks with great vivacity on all possible subjects under the sun. Broadly speaking he is a general merchant of all kinds of ideas but he knows how to sell his wares; he sells them like a businessman. Shaw's intelligence is *par excellence*. His intellect is a high-functioning-dynamo and the ideas which pass through it acquire a unique charge. He has nothing to do with the artist's intuition; that is not his domain.

His application to the problem of our daily life is exuberant and vigorous. He grapples with ideas fiercely and shapes them to fit in the framework of art. He does not seem loyal to art, he is loyal only to society.

But Shaw is a revolutionary more in theory than in practice. He does not believe in revolutionary measures. In his play *Candida* he is more candid when he marshalls out his ideas through Marchbank. Marchbank talks intelligently and profoundly on the injustice perpetrated upon the different, sections of society, but in his conduct he is only a status ghost. Tanner's *The Revolutionary Handbook* is more a collection of high sounding maxims than a programme for a fundamental change in society.

Shaw gave a new force to English drama which it had lacked in the hands of Arthur Henry Jones and Cicero. He did not only create the new drama of the twentieth century, the drama of ideas and problems, but also prepared the audience to accord it a hearty welcome. But perhaps the predominant influence that urged him to turn to the drama was the success of Ibsen, the Norwegian dramatist, who seemed to him a parallel genius.

Shaw had certain ideas to present before the public through the medium of his plays. He saw things as they are and had the courage to tell it frankly in a constructive language. He thought not to acknowledge ready-made opinions. He set his mind free from prejudice, presupposition, superstitution, illusion and popular delusion. He had his own thought on the current burning problems of humanity at large. He saw things as they were and eschewed the jaundiced approach. He refused to be carried away by emotion. He fervently put forth his ideas into his plays and hoped to convert people to his own way of thinking. Each play of Shaw presents a definite original idea of Shaw himself. He projects his own personality into several of the characters. Though drama is a compound art, he did not keep himself aloof from his plays altogether. He never bothered about the glorification of art for the sake of art. He had no conception of drama as a literary form in which the meaning is achieved through the total pattern and by the language put in the mouths of characters. This is well-confirmed by his stage direction, in which not only the actions of characters, but their state of mind also is well-expressed. It was Shaw's greatness that he gave the air of seriousness and purposiveness to drama without sacrificing the element of fun and gaiety that the audience so earnestly longed for. He gave his philosophical pills a nice sugar coating.

Shaw had at heart a bent for satire. He could not write a sympathetic note on the life of London as in *David Copperfield* but he would pen satires burning with indignation like the *Widower's House*. If Shaw had lived in the days of Alexander Pope, he would probably have written verse but as he lived in the days of Oscar Wilde and the epigrammatic stage he wrote plays, particularly comedies. His satiric genius gave a tilt to his dramatic art and made him a comedian rather than a tragedian. Shaw asserts "Art for arts sake is not enough; for art sake alone I would not face the toil of writing a single sentence."[1] He made his literary faculty subordinate to a moral purpose. He became a crusader whose mission was to restore colour and light to England's once green and pleasant land. In *Man and Superman* Tanner says:

> I have become a reformer and like all reformers and iconoclast, I no longer break cucumber frames and burn glass bushes. I shatter creeds and demolish ideals.[2]

---

1. G.B. Shaw: *Man and Superman,* Penguin Books Limited, Australia, 1975, p. 35.
2. *Ibid.*, p. 74.

The giants at which he tilts, says Cotte James, are moral slavery, humbug mental sloth, social apathy, superstition, sentimentalism, collective selfishness and all the static ideas which have not been consciously subjected to the taste of the real life and honest thought. Shaw was not merely satisfied by demolishing old values. He is the great destroyer of evils in modern age and out of his destructiveness, he seeks to take us towards a better destiny. He had to remain a propagandist for certain of his ideas which he used to nourish in his practical life. In some of his plays he is neither a reformer nor a propagandist. *In You Never Can Tell*, for instance, he is preoccupied providing entertainment to the reader. He was the cheering, zestful, greathearted veteran who had the flavour of the battle of wits.

The conflicts constantly rising in the soul of Shaw between opposite elements demanded an objective treatment and for that purpose drama was the best medium. He believed that stage was the best medium for discussion and dissemination of ideas. Since he had many things to say to his generation he used the theatre as the vehicle of his thought. He accepted the theatre and used it for the purpose of discussion.

Shaw belonged to an unconventional group of artists. It is in this sense that he is a specialist of new kind of surgery. He considers life from a guardian's viewpoint. He is strong enough to meet the challenge of truth. Shaw's dramatic career marks an advance in ideas over that of Ibsen. In his search for the essence of reality, Shaw has to shatter to pieces the veil of romance and the institution of respectability. But, in spite of everything, he is a confused thinker.

G.B. Shaw was born in Dublin in 1856. He was very shy but he created the persona of G.B.S., the showman satirist, controversialist, critic, pundit, wit, intellectual buffoon and dramatist. The term Shavian was coined in his honour on account of his brilliant qualities. After his arrival in London in 1876 he became an active socialist and a brilliant platform speaker. He received his education at the British museum and, consequently, became intensely and keenly interested in cultural subjects. He made an attack on the London theatre and became closely associated with the intellectual revival of the British theatre. His mother was very fond of music and art and it enabled him to register her musical impact in his plays. Shaw was not lucky enough to receive a good education due to poverty. By nature he was a joker and he used to tell very serious things even in the way of joking. He was a rebel like Shelley and he rebels against the social corruption mounting very high at his time.

One aspect of his life and character needs to be emphasised more than any other aspect. He was before his marriage, a Don Juan in his relations with women. Before his marriage he was attached to so many women although women for him had no primary importance. He philandered with his worshippers and from his contact with them, he tried to find out material for his works. The first Act of *Philanderer* is a transcript of an experience which Shaw has acknowledged. He wrote novels such as Immaturity, *The Irrational Knot, Love among* the Artists etc. He thinks that the family ideal is an apple of discord and a humbug. Parents and children in his works seem to be incompetent to live together. He desires to strike the note that youth and age cannot see eye to eye with each other. The natural revolt of the children is well noticed in his novel *Immaturity* and in his play *Mrs. Warren's Profession.*

The failure of Shaw as a critic turned him to the field of drama which was the best medium for the expression of his ideas. The subjective conflict constantly rising and falling in his mind between opposite elements, egoism and socialism, intellect and instinct, reason and emotion demanded an objective kind of treatment and for that purpose drama was the best medium.

His family was always in debt due to his father's fondness for liquor which Shaw disliked. He had to leave school at the age of fifteen and work as a clerk. Five years later he left the job and came to London to live with his mother and sister who were merely staying away from the father. The mother supported the family by giving lesson in music to school girls. It was around this time that he had his first affair with Mrs. Jenny Patterson, a widow who used to take singing lessons from his mother. The affair started when she invited him to tea and ruthlessly seduced him. "I permitted her" says Shaw, "being intensely curious on the subject." The affair lasted for a few years. Shaw was extremely jealous and at no time could she bear him flirting with other women. Moreover, by this time, he had become a confirmed philanderer. The next woman who stepped into his life was an actress named Florence Farr. He found her a pleasant change after his none too pleasant experience with the aggressive widow. Besides being good looking and clever, Florence Farr treated sex very casually which was exactly what Shaw desired. She was not susceptible to jealousy because Shaw was not her only lover. By 1894 it was said that she had as many as fourteen lovers on her list. From this experience Shaw concluded that sex was hopeless as a bond for a permanent relation.

The British Museum was Shaw's second home at that time. Here he met Eleaner the youngest daughter of Karl Marx, the celebrated German socialist and philosopher. When they encountered each other everyday in the reading room, it was but natural that they developed amorous relationship. Shaw went even to the extent of trying with Marxism just as their relations were mounting up but suddenly their ties snapped. Shaw had no comments to offer. After all "all is fair in love and war." "The ideal love affair is one conducted by post", said Shaw.[1] "My correspondence with actress Ellen Terry was a wholly satisfactory love affair. I could have met her at any time but I did not want to complicate such a delightful relationship. She got tired of five husbands but she never got tired of me. My relations with Patrick Campbell were as innocent as those of King Magnus in *The Apple Cart*,"[2] He came in contact with Annie Besant and developed a romantic relationship with her. It is interesting that she was the very same Mrs. Annie Besant who in 1914 joined the Indian National Congress and championed the cause of India's freedom by forming the Home Rule League movement. At the time Shaw came to know her, he had already earned a name as the finest orator of his generation Annie Besant had started her career by propagating atheism under the influence of Bradlaugh, evolution under Edward Aveling, Socialism under Shaw and finally Theosophy under the influence of Madam Blavetsky. On the first meeting Annie Besant was hardly impressed with Shaw. Here was a rare case of love not at first sight but on second thought. It could have been mainly because her humourless nature was utterly unlike his. He was capable of laughing at anything and she at nothing. But there was something in Shaw which finally swept her off her feet. By the spring of 1885 she was head over heels in love with him. Annie Besant invited Shaw to spend his evening at her house in Avenue Road, where they played Piano. She also agreed to serialise his rejected novels in her magazine 'Our corner' and even paid for his contributions from her private account.

Though Annie Besant could hold any audience spellbound by her magnificent oratory, her hold on Shaw was very tenuous. He found her extremely dull. She insisted that their relations be put on a serious

1. J.C. Jain, *Mirror*, Sons Vartaman Press, Bombay, 1978, p. 35.
2. *Ibid*.

footing. Since her husband was very much alive and kicking, she could not marry Shaw. So she made a contact setting forth the terms on which they were to live together as man and wife and presented it to him for signature. "Good God!" he exclaimed; "This is worse than all the vows of all the churches on the earth. I would rather be legally married to you ten times over."[1] About his love-affairs Shaw confessed that he mostly philandered with women to get material for his plays that were to make him famous. Hence Raina in *Arms and the Man* is Annie Besant, Jullia in *The Philanderer* is Mrs. Jenny Patterson, and so on and so forth. Most of the women in his plays are the women he had once known.

Shaw's adventures in the realm of romance came almost to an end in the summer of 1896, when he met his future wife Charllote Pyne Townshend. She was not simply wealthy but also very intelligent. For all practical purposes she was a good catch. It was a long romance lasting for two years. Shaw was still not out of the woods as he was earning little as a musician and dramatic critic for 'The Saturday Review'. But he was no longer the obscure personality that he was twenty years back. He was already treading on the road of fame and fortune. On June 1, 1898 Shaw and Charlotte became husband and wife. But marriage did in no way put an end to his epistolary love-affairs which continued for years. He not only kept writing letters but even went on receiving letters from women. Shaw's marriage with Charlotte was a happy one. He exclaimed: "There are two tragedies in life. One is to lose your heartly desire. The other is to gain it."[2]

She could not get any institutional training either in the field of journalism or play-writing. He developed his sense of writing due to his lust for social engineering. In the beginning of his career he was a writer without a serious moral purpose, a light-hearted iconoclast but today he is big enough to deserve from any authority, a certificate of a serious thinker in the school of thinkers. But his early life was not a pleasant one. In a letter to Ellen Terry, when he was above forty, he summed up his childhood in a pregnant reference:

Oh, a devil of childhood, Ellen, rich only in dreams, frightful and loveless in reality.[3]

---

1. *Ibid.*, p. 90.
2. G.B. Shaw: *Man and Superman, op. cit.*, p. 208.
3. St. John Ervine: *Bernard Shaw: His Life, Work and Friends,* William Morrow & Co., New York, 1956, p. 90.

The formative years of Shaw were spent in adverse circumstances. His blood was bourgeois blood. St. John Ervine writes, "It may be pointed out that Shaw was an affectionate son and looked after his mother till the last day of her life."[1] Shaw seems to have never thought to achieve eminence as a writer. But there was a sub-conscious urge for literary expression even from his childhood. He kept himself engaged in letter-writing throughout his career. When in 1875 two American evangelists visited Dublin, he took deep interest in religious movements and controversies, wrote a letter which was published on 3rd April, 1875. In the letter, he protested against revivalism, partly anticipating his later on slaught on sentimental Christianity in preface to *Androcles and the Lion*.

Shaw as a philosopher was interested in bringing about changes in the thinking, the life and the environment of man. The precondition of this was a philosophical rejuvenation of the people as a whole and the creation of the spirit of adventure and the ability to face obstacles. Shaw was aware that philosophers normally think of only the ultimate objectives and therefore, are likely to lose touch with the day-to-day world and its problems. He was against nurturing a philosophy which concentrated on the ultimate objectives, leaving man and his problems neglected. In philosophy and metaphysics, the problems are more remote, less transient and less connected with our day's routine. Probably he insists that a living philosophy must answer the problems of the day.

Shaw had a scientific approach to the problems of life. He combined his scientific fervour with a deep respect. Change is a must for the betterment of the human race. His concept of superman requires an absolute change, change in the selection of sex, change in social and political conditions. He does not divorce the past because to deny the past and break with it completely is to uproot ourselves. His concept and philosophy of superman is to be viewed in the context of his desire to imbibe the good things of the past. Ramsden speaks partly for his creator when he says:

> Execuse me, Octavius; but there are limits to social toleration. You know that I am not a bigoted or prejudiced man. You know that I am plain Roebuck Ramsden when other men who have done less have got handles to their names, because I have stood for equality and liberty of conscience while they were

1. *Ibid.*, p. 369.

> truckling to the Church and to the aristocracy. Whitefield and I lost chance after chance through our advanced opinions. But I draw the line at Anarchism and Free Love and that sort of thing. If I am to be Annie's guardian, she will have to learn that she has a duty to me. I wont have: I will not have it. She must forbid John Tanner the house; and so must you.[1]

Shaw in retrospect is linked with H.G. Wells. Truly speaking, he was an embattled socialist and evolutionist debating endlessly on platform and in print. He was influenced by the four masters of youth: Bunyan, Blake, Dickens, and Ruskin. But he was no less influenced by Plato and Nietzsche when he pleaded for the evolution of man into superman. As a matter of fact, the influences on Shaw are numerous, and there appears to have been a new one behind every new idea that he took up.

1. G.B. Shaw: *Man and Superman*, *op. cit.*, p. 46.

II

The Sapling

Shaw appears to have taken the idea of the superman from Nietzsche, though both regarding the process of creation of the superman, and his concept of him, he differs materially from the latter. Nietzsche's superman is endowed neither with a life-span of one thousand years nor with the power of creating human dolls, nor does he come out of an egg. "Nietzsche had said that just as the ape ultimately produced the man, so should we ultimately made a something higher than the man. The immediate answer, of course, is sufficiently obvious: the ape did not worry about the man, so why should we worry about the superman? If the superman will come by natural selection, may we leave it to natural selection? If the superman will come by human selection, what sort of superman are we to select? If he is simply to be more just, more brave, or more merciful, then Zarathustra sinks into a Sunday-school teacher: the only way we can work for it is to be more just, more brave, and more merciful; sensible advice, but hardly startling. If he is to be anything else than this, why should we desire him, or what else are we to desire? These questions have been many times asked of the Nietzscheites, and none of the Nietzscheites even attempted to answer them."[1]

Shaw furthered the idea and provided a definite plan according to which, in his opinion, the birth of the superman took place. He evolved the concept of Life-Force which, according to him, was at the root of all creation and which was ultimately to bring about the birth of the superman. In *Man and Superman* he not only gives a lucid illustration of the concept through the story but also supplies a philosophical exposition of it through the statements made by several of the characters, especially Tanner and Don Juan.

---

1. G.K. Chesterton: *George Bernard Shaw*, Guild Books, London, W.C.I., 1951, p. 88.

The Life-Force, says Tanner, acts primarily through woman who makes man a tool of the great purpose of nature. "Vitality in a woman is a blind fury of creation. She sacrifices herself to it", and she will not hesitate to sacrifice her man. But man is not the escaping, the fleeing party. He becomes a helpless agent in the power of Life-Force and does what Life-Force directs him to do. Don Juan tells Ann:

> In the sex relation the universal creative energy, of which the parties are both the helpless agents, overrides and sweeps away all personal considerations, and dispenses with all personal relations. The pair, may be utter strangers to one another, speaking different languages, differing in race and colour, in age and disposition, with no bond between them but a possibility of that fecundity for the sake of which the Life-Force throws them into one another's arms at the exchange of a glance. Do we not recognise this by allowing marriages to be made by parents without consulting the woman?[1]

The Life-Force works not only in the sphere of the perpetuation of the race but also contributes to the betterment of it. The ploughman is satisfied with his lot; he "eats more, sleeps better, and rejoices in the wife of his bosom with less misgiving" than the philosopher. But the philosopher would not like to exchange his life with that of the ploughman. This is because the philosopher is in the grip of the Life-Force. This Life-Force says to him, "I have done a thousand wonderful willing to live and following the line of least resistance: now I want to know myself and my destination, and choose my path; so I have made a special brain – a philosopher's brain – to grasp this knowledge for me as the husbandman's hand grasps the plough for me. And this, says the Life-Force to the philosopher, "must thou strive to do for me until thou diest, when I will make another brain and another philosopher to carry on the work".[2]

The Life-Force acts as a selecting agent also and brings the better men and the better women together for the procreation of a still better race. A perpetual war has been going on between Life on one side and Death and Degeneration on the other, and Life's continuous effort has been "not only to maintain itself, but to achieve higher and higher

1. G.B. Shaw: *Man and Superman,* Penguin Books Harmondsworth, 1951, p. 171.
2. *Ibid.*, p. 179.

organization and complete self-consciousness". In Life's effort "to achieve higher and higher organisation and completes self-consciousness", both man and woman act as unconscious tools. Woman knows by instinct that she needs man, though it was she who created him, "in order to produce something better than the single-sexed process can produce."[1] Man, on the other hand, acts as a willing tool.

Does man really desire to have superman or to grow into a superman himself? Does the democratic system of government need superman? Will not the presence of superman in a society, where everyone is theoretically equal to everyone else, unbalance the system itself? G.B. Shaw answers these questions in *The Revolutionist's Handbook* and *Pocket Companion* purported to have been written by John Tanner, Member of the Idle Rich Class. Tanner Writes:

> Man does desire an ideal Superman with such energy as he can spare from his nutrition, and has in every age magnified the best living substitute for it he can find. His last incompetent general is set up as an Alexander; his King is the first gentleman in the world; His Pope is a saint. He is never without an array of human idols who are all nothing but sham Supermen.[2]

As a matter of fact the desire to have supermen amidst us is so great that we ignore the danger that the presence of such individuals involves for our cherished ideals of "right, duty, honour, justice, religion, even decency". Man today is blind to the trampling of these ideals even by casual "Supermen" like a Caesar or Napoleon. "He will, therefore, make no objection to the production of a race of what he calls Great men or Heroes, because he will imagine them, not true Supermen, but as himself endowed with infinite brains, infinite courage, and infinite money."[3]

The ideal of political equality has grown so popular today that people may dislike the idea of being congenitally inferior to others. But the "Proletarian Democracy" that we have evolved today has failed miserably to provide a solution of the innumerable social and other allied problems that we are confronted with. The old systems of government which have been replaced by Proletarian Democracy "depended on the existence of Supermen acting as despots or oligarchs; and not only were these

1. *Ibid.*, p. 157.
2. *Ibid.*, p. 240.
3. *Ibid.*

Supermen not always or even often forthcoming at the right moment or in an eligible social position, but when they were forthcoming they could not, except for a short time and by morally suicidal coercive methods, impose superhumanity on those whom they governed...."[1]

Thus the really efficient governments have been the governments run by supermen, and the idea of "Proletarian Democracy", of equality to all in the matters of government, was born only when supermen were not available to rescue the people at the right moment. But the experience of democracy has, according to Tanner, shown that in it the government is bound to pass into the hands of rogues and crooks. So the real salvation of humanity lies in having supermen available at all moments of crisis, or still better, in having a democracy of supermen itself. Political exigency demands that we should produce supermen.

In *Man and Superman* Shaw emphasised the role of Life-Force in the birth of the superman by pointing out that it brings superior men and superior women together and thus helps in the improvement of the race. In *Back to Methuselah*, written about twenty years later, he adds another concept, the concept of Creative Evolution, which is supposed to have no less important a part than Life-Force in the evolution of the Superman. He defines Creative Evolution in the following words:

> But this dismal creed (that evolution is the result of an accident) does not discourage those who believe that the impulse that produces evolution is creative. They have observed the simple part that the will to do anything can and does, at a certain pitch of intensity set up by conviction of its necessity, create and organise new tissue to do it with. To them, therefore, mankind is, by no means, played out yet. If the weight lifter, under the trivial stimulus of an athletic competition, can "put up a muscle", it seems reasonable to believe that an equally earnest and convinced philosopher could "put up a brain". Both are directions of vitality to a certain end. Evolution shews us this direction of vitality doing all sorts of things: providing the centipede with a hundred legs, and ridding the fish of any legs at all; building lungs and arms for the land and gins and fins for the sea; enabling the mammal to gestate its young inside its body, and the fowl to incubate hers outside it; offering us,

1. *Ibid.*, p. 242.

> we may say, our choice of any sort of bodily contrivance to maintain our activity and increase our resources.[1]

The concept of Creative Evolution is not a negation of the concept of Life-Force; it is only an improvement upon and addition to it. Life-Force is at the root of all creation of life, while Creative Evolution is the cause of every improvement that takes place in a living organism. At the initial stage Creative Evolution acts by itself, without the conscious association of the being or the organism concerned, and then it is somewhat identical with Darwin's concept of Survival of the Fittest. But at an advanced stage it is a force consciously used by the being or the organism concerned; it is, at this stage, both a force of, and a plan for, a change for the better.

The desire for change was born in Adam's mind when he found that he would have to live for ever. The prospect of an eternal life horrified him when he found that the perpetuation of life was an end in itself. He said to Eve:

> I want to be different; to be better; to being again and again; to shed myself as a snake sheds its skin. I am tired of myself. And yet I must endue myself, not for a day or for many days, but for ever. That is a dreadful thought. That is what makes me sit broading and silent and hateful.[2]

The desire for change is the motivating force behind Creative Evolution. It is similar to Life-Force, but it is not identical with the latter. Life-Force is more a product of the blood and the flesh than of the brain. The desire to renew itself is ingrained in the constitution of a living being and when one has learnt to conquer death through birth, death loses a part of its terror; and, as the serpent says:

> Death is not an unhappy thing when you have learnt how to conquer it.[3]

When this desire for a change for the better grips the mind, Life-Force changes into Creative Evolution. The desire for change stirs the imagination, and imagination, acting as the agent of Creative Evolution, creates and evolves the species. The serpent informs Eve that Lilith, the

1. Bernard Shaw: *Complete Plays With Prefaces*, Vol. II, Dodd, Mead & Co., New York, 1962, p. xviii.
2. *Ibid.*, p. 5.
3. *Ibid.*, p. 7.

mother of Adam and Eve, created the latter without the help of a male partner by the sheer force of imagination.

> You imagine what you desire; you will what you imagine; and at last you create what you will.[1]

Eve took the serpent's advice and, with the help of Adam, produced children and thus death was finally conquered. There would now be no end of the human race even if Adam and Eve died. This was the first step towards the evolution of the human race into a better race. But the idea of the superman first took hold of Cain who was not satisfied with just being a tiller of the soil like his father. When Eve upbraids him for being the murderer of his brother and for turning his wife Lua into an idler, Cain twirls his moustache proudly and says that he had made of himself a superman:

> There is something higher than man.
> There is hero and superman.[2]

Eve is scandalised and says:

> Superman! You are no superman! You are Anti-man; You are to other men what the stoat is to the rabbit, and she is to you what the leech is to the stoat. You despise your father; but when he dies the world will be the richer because he lived. When you dies, men will say, "He was a great warrior; but if he had never been born." And of Lua they will say nothing; but when they think of her' they will spit.[3]

It is clear that Eve's ideal man is different from that of Cain. Eve was satisfied with ordinary toiler who spends his days in attending to his daily routine and earning the daily bread for his family. Cain on the other hand, plans to be extraordinary. He thinks that he is justified in aspiring to be extraordinary because he would, thereby, become different from beasts. He tells Adam:

> I revolt against the clay. I revolt against the food. You say it gives us strength; does it not also turn into filth and smite us with diseases? I revolt against these births that you and

1. *Ibid.*, p. 10.
2. *Ibid.*, p. 24.
3. *Ibid.*

> mother are proud of. They drag us down to the level of beasts. If that is the last things as if has been the first, let mankind perish. If I am to act like a bear, if Lua is to bring forth cubs like a bear, then I had rather be a bear than a man; for the bear is not ashamed; he knows no better. If you content, like the bear, I am not.[1]

A superman is, moreover, feared by others and no one has the courage to harm him. Even if he does things that others, do not approve of, no one can dare stand against him because he belongs to a category of his own and the ordinary norms of good and bad, right and wrong, do not apply to him:

> "It is said , says Cain to Adam, "that my deed was as a mark on me, a burnt-in mark such as Abel put on his sheep, that no man should slay me. And here I stand unslain, whilst the cowards who have never slain, the men who are content to be their brothers' keepers instead of their masters, are despised and rejected and slain like rabbits. He who bears the brand of Cain shall rule the earth.[2]

Cain thinks he is superman, or at least he has decided to be considered a superman, but he is not the superman that ultimately emerges in the last book of the Pentateuch. He is a superman of the same breed to which despots and oligarchs belonged. Shaw did not, and could not think of him as his ideal superman, and Cain's ambitions are being emphasised only to illustrate that the desire to be out of the ordinary was present in man's mind from at the earliest stage of his creation, and this desire inflamed his imagination and the result was the gradual evolution in the race of man. Cain's desire to be better than, and superior to, his father sets Eve's imagination on wings and she also dreams of the day when man will get release from the necessity of toiling for breed:

> Man need not always live by bread alone, There is something else. We do not yet know what it is; but some day we shall find out; and then we wall live on that alone; and there shall be no more digging nor spinning, nor fighting nor killing.[3]

1. *Ibid.*, p. 29.
2. *Ibid.*, p. 26.
3. *Ibid.*, p. 34.

Shaw is beyond any 'ism' but still the fact remains that his rendering of ideas enables us to call him a thinker. The cause of Shaw's changing philosophy is not his confused approach but the impact of social changes on his thoughts. His superman is a necessity for the entire humanity. He repeatedly hammers on the point that the creation of the superman is not possible in social disparity because disparity breeds violence in society and wastes opportunities of the people in society and this will only hamper the birth of the superman. His concept of superman is not a flight of imagination because it is based on realistic idealism. His concept of superman is not the cry of a mad man. The Statue in *Man and Superman* says:

> Superman is a good cry; and a good cry is half the battle. I should like to see this Nietzsche.[1]

Shaw's theory of Life-Force and his concept of superman can operate only in social and political equality. Plato's new man was an utopean creature but Shaw's superman is to be evolved according to the laws of biology. In *Man and Superman*, Shaw propounds the concept of superman and gives a hint that the Superman can be produced by the help of two intellectual persons consisting of a male and female. If the superman is to be born, he must be born from the womb of a woman. Plato, the ideal thinker hoped to see the superman only by the help of selective breeding but Shaw, unlike Plato, views that the birth of superman requires an absolute change in the social and political disparity along with selection in breeding. Intellectual male and female combined together alone can produce the superman but only in the equilibrium of socialism. He did not brush aside social disparity because he thought it would create an obstacle in the birth of the superman. Social and political changes are a basic demand for the creation of the superman. Thus, evolution towards superman involves a basic reorientation of social, economic, political and biological priorities which is what Shaw's evolutionary stands for.

Shaw attacks the system of marriage because it is a hindrance in the way of the creation of the superman. He pleaded in his plays like *Heart Break House, Getting Married* and *Mrs. Warren's Profession* to abrogate the institution of marriage. Marriage in his view is legalised prostitution and it is not conducive for the birth of the superman. He emphasises in his play *Candida* that marriage is no guarantee of love which goes

1. G.B. Shaw: *Man and Superman*, Penguin Books Ltd., Australia, p. 172.

to help in the birth of the superman. Candida does not surrender to a romantic fool like Marchbank because he will make a bad husband and ultimately the birth of superman will be blocked. This involves a sturdy realism of a woman's awareness of practical necessities like wealth, respectability, opportunities for saving and educating children, which are no less important than the biology of evolution. Unlike, *A Doll's House* of Isben's in which Nora leaves her husband along with her children, Candida in the similar situation does not walk out of her house and it shows a wise step on her part. Shaw is an economist and creative evolutionist and his politics is only a hyphen between his economic and evolutionary doctrines. He had a faith in the natural evolution from the very beginning but when the went on writing his *Man and Superman*, his faith in the natural process came to an end. After loosing his faith in the doctrine of natural evolution, he put his faith in the theory of Life-Force which helps in the constitution of the superman. His faith in the biblical theory of creation appears to be lost in his play *Man and Superman*. But it is recovered in his *Back to Methuselah*. The elderly gentleman says:

> My body is dust, Madam: not soul. What does it matter what my body is made of? The dust of the ground, the particles of the air, or even the slime of the ditch? The important thing is that when my creator took it, whenever it was he breathed into its nostril the breath of life; and man became a living soul. Yes Madam, a living soul. I am not the dust of the ground. I am a living soul that is an exalting, a magnificent thought, it is also a great scientific fact.[1]

Shaw was not torn between chaos and confusion like Tennyson who also posed as a prophet and thinker. Shaw did not rely on the Bible because it has a little function to perform in the birth of the superman. He discarded the religion of his forefathers and worked to bring a better world into being. He felt that need for a credible and healthy religion based on natural, scientific history in the place of the supernatural one that had definitely crumbled. He is not of the view like Darwin that man is the son of a monkey but, unlike him, he holds that man is the product of sexual intercourse between a man and a woman. Unlike D.H. Lawrence, Shaw places importance on the intellectual aspect of his characters that supplements and fulfils their biological sole. His female characters do

1. G.B. Shaw: *Back to Methuselah*. Vol. II. Dodd. Mead & Co. New York, 1962, p. 156.

not marry romantic fools and unintellectual persons because they are incompetent to prove good husbands.

Shaw insists on the necessity of education which will assist to in the birth of the superman. In Mrs. Warren's Profession, Shaw explores the theme of prostitution resulting out of poverty but along with the exploration of the theme of prostitution, he also emphasises the need of education. Mrs. Warren provides a better education to her child Vivie by engaging herself in the game of prostitution. He could not stick to any single problem, rather he left no stone unturned to touch every problem confronting society which acted as an obstacle in the birth of superman.

Lamarck postulated that great changes in atmosphere necessarily result in changes in the needs of animals; their altered needs induce the animals to make some efforts which result in altered habits and these altered habits produce structural changes from use or disuse of particular organs. There is a fundamental difference between Lamarck's theory and Darwin's theory. Although Darwin professed ignorance about the causes of variations, he laid emphasis on direct and definite action of external conditions and chance as two important factors of variations. Lamarck's theory boldly starts from the consideration that animals chose, by an assertion of the will, to conduct their lives in a certain manner. According to Darwin the main cause of variation is the direct action of changed conditions of existence, while with Lamarck the action of the conditions of existence is indirect, the direct action being that of the animals themselves, in consequence of changed sense of need under changed conditions. Lamarck does not attribute to the physical environment any direct transforming action on the form of species but recognises in the living being the power of varying according to needs. Lamarck's theory is not deterministic and mechanistic like Darwin's. On the other hand, Lamarck did not formulate a complete and perfect system. His theory is not adequate enough to account for the evolution of the superman.

The difference between Lamarck's approach and Butler's approach is not of kind but of degree. According to both, purpose, will, effort and heredity are the indispensable conditions that operate in the evolution of species. Bulter's concept of heredity is different from that of Lamarck, Lamarck emphasises the effect of environment which is inherited and passed on to the next generation but he does not link on the experiences of the race to that of the individual. He held that life originated from dead matter by a process of spontaneous generation while Butler looked upon the so-called inorganic world as living up to a certain point. Shaw has championed both Lamarck and Butler. But it was in the work of the latter that he found the basic clue to his doctrine of Creative Evolution.

Shaw is a staunch supporter of Creative Evolution. The idea of Creative Evolution is referred to here and there in his early writings. But it was in the dream episode in Act III of *Man and Superman* that he makes a conscious and consistent statement. The Devil says about Nietzsche:

> Well, he came here first, before he recovered his wits. I had some hopes of him; but he was a confirmed Life-Force worshipper. It was he who raked up the Superman, who is as old as Prometheus; and the 10th century will run after this newest of the old crazes when it gets tired of the world, the flesh, and your humble servant.[1]

The Statue then remaks:

> Superman is a good cry; and a good cry is half the battle. I should like to see this Nietzsche.[2]

The third Act of *Man and Superman* along with *A Revolutionist's Handbook* confirms the essence of Shaw's philosophy of the superman. Don Juan, who is Shaw's spokesman, covers that happiness does not count in life. He is bored with his life in hell, the home of the unreal and the seekers of happiness. Life is the only truth in his view and proclaims that his purpose of going to Heaven, the home of the masters of reality, is to escape from the vulgar pursuit of happiness.

It is interesting here to note that Shaw lost his faith in Christianity and renounced God early in his life and yet he is a deeply religious man. Shaw's God is Life-Force which can create a superman. The Life-Force, says Don Juan in *Man and Superman*, is the creative power behind the creation of the superman. The progressive growth of species from amoebe to man is progress. The Life-Force has purpose but its ultimate purpose is quite unknown. It seems that Life-Force has a passion for social engineering and it creates only to satisfy this urge and its creations are different stages rather than final achievements. Man is superior to all species so far evolved by the Life-Force. But the fact remains that man is not the last stage in the process of evolution. Evolution is creative.

1. *Man and Superman, op. cit.*, p. 172.
2. *Ibid.*

Shaw's Life-Force is not a particular sect of religion in the strict sense of the term. He looks upon woman as life incarnate. Woman created man for the sole purpose of her own impregnation because a double sex process of procreation is more economical than a single sex process. It is the woman who takes the initiative in the process of creation. The blind attempt to pursue a man by a woman in *Man and Superman* constitutes the gist of comedy but it also brings to focus the philosophy of Shaw. He gives a particular status to woman in the process of the evolution of the super race. Her predominant function is to produce the human race and to preserve it. Her death will be the sign of universal death. The single purpose of her life is to carry out her mission. Tanner says:

> It is the self-sacrificing woman that sacrifices others most recklessly. Because they are unselfish, they are kind in little things. Because they have a purpose which is not their own purpose, but that of the whole universe, a man is nothing to them but an instrument of that purpose.[1]

Motherhood is a life long cherished desire of a woman and it is but natural that she will not let her purpose go in vain. Ann ceases to be the mere heroine of a facial comedy, for she is inclined for sexual pleasure but accomplishment of the purpose of the Life-Force which desires that men and women should cooperate to bring into being a better race. By submitting to the purpose of Ann, Tanner becomes the tool of Life-Force because, therefore, he becomes an instrument to do his share for the future of the race. Ann and Tanner both embrace Shaw's religion because both dedicate themselves to a purpose which is not their own purpose but of the whole universe.

The philosopher is something more than a mere tool of woman's purpose. Woman is the embodiment of Life-Force while the philosopher symbolises its intellectual consciousness; woman creates and preserves life while the philosopher attaches value to it. Woman perpetuates the species while the man of genius improves its quality by conceiving something better by pointing out the direction of what it may be. It seems that Shaw passes a censure against Christianity's gospel by holding his view that we are not in the hands of God, but God is in our hands. Man must try to evolve into superman and assume control of the rudder of evolution.

1. *Ibid.*, p. 61.

Marriage delays the birth of the superman. Shaw demands nothing less than the abrogation of the present necessary association of marriage with conjugation. Conjugation is inevitable to nothing but the propagation of the race. The birth of superman also demands the abolition of social classes. It is impossible unless the social gulf is bridged up. Shaw says in the *The Revolutionists Handbook:*

> Until there is an England in which every man is a Cromwell, a France in which every man is a Napoleon, a Rome in which every man is a Caesar, a Germany in which every man is a Luther plus a Goethe, the world will be no more improved by its heroes than a Brixton villa is improved by the pyramid of Cheops. The production of such nations is the only real change possible to us.[1]

Mrs. Warren's Profession, though not a sex drama, reveals one aspect of the sex instinct. It shows that sanguinity does not count between strangers. Frank Gardner and Vivie Warren are attracted to each other, although they are half brother and half sister. This shows that Shaw was influenced by Ibsen's Ghosts in which Oswald Alving and Regina Engstrand who are half brother and half sister and are found in the closest situation.

Shaw's second play *The Philanderer* is the first play to deal with sex and marriage. To Shaw marriage is an institution which society has outgrown but not modified. But in this play he had failed to give a clear-cut picture of modified marriage. In reality, he wanted to abolish the system of marriage. Blanche expresses her antipathy to marriage in the following words addressed to her father:

> Then I will not marry him. He has played fast and loose with me. He thinks us beneath him: he is ashamed of us: he dared to object to being benefited by you as if it were not natural for him to owe you everything; and yet the money tempted him after all. Papa: I do not want to marry: I only want to stay with you and be happy as we have always been. I hate the thought of being married: I dont care for him: I dont want to leave you.[2]

1. *Ibid.*, p. 225.
2. G.B. Shaw: *Plays Unpleasant,* Penguin Books Ltd., Australia , 1960, p. 77.

Marriage delays the birth of the superman. Shaw demands nothing than the abrogation of the present necessary association of marriage 1 conjugation. Conjugation is inevitable to nothing but the propagation he race. The birth of superman also demands the abolition of social ses. It is impossible unless the social gulf is bridged up. Shaw says in The Revolutionists Handbook:

> Until there is an England in which every man is a Cromwell, a France in which every man is a Napoleon, a Rome in which every man is a Caesar, a Germany in which every man is a Luther plus a Goethe, the world will be no more improved by its heroes than a Brixton villa is improved by the pyramid of Cheops. The production of such nations is the only real change possible to us.[1]

Irs. Warren's Profession, though not a sex drama, reveals one aspect sex instinct. It shows that sanguinity does not count between ers. Frank Gardner and Vivie Warren are attracted to each other, gh they are half brother and half sister. This shows that Shaw fluenced by Ibsen's Ghosts in which Oswald Alving and Regina and who are half brother and half sister and are found in the situation.

aw's second play *The Philanderer* is the first play to deal with l marriage. To Shaw marriage is an institution which society has vn but not modified. But in this play he had failed to give a clear-ure of modified marriage. In reality, he wanted to abolish the of marriage. Blanche expresses her antipathy to marriage in the g words addressed to her father:

> hen I will not marry him. He has played fast and loose with e. He thinks us beneath him: he is ashamed of us: he dared object to being benefited by you as if it were not natural for n to owe you everything; and yet the money tempted him er all. Papa: I do not want to marry: I only want to stay with 1 and be happy as we have always been. I hate the thought of ng married: I dont care for him: I dont want to leave you.[2]

225.

aw: *Plays Unpleasant,* Penguin Books Ltd., Australia , 1960, p. 77.

not marry romantic fools and unintellectual persons because they are incompetent to prove good husbands.

Shaw insists on the necessity of education which will assist to in the birth of the superman. In Mrs. Warren's Profession, Shaw explores the theme of prostitution resulting out of poverty but along with the exploration of the theme of prostitution, he also emphasises the need of education. Mrs. Warren provides a better education to her child Vivie by engaging herself in the game of prostitution. He could not stick to any single problem, rather he left no stone unturned to touch every problem confronting society which acted as an obstacle in the birth of superman.

Lamarck postulated that great changes in atmosphere necessarily result in changes in the needs of animals; their altered needs induce the animals to make some efforts which result in altered habits and these altered habits produce structural changes from use or disuse of particular organs. There is a fundamental difference between Lamarck's theory and Darwin's theory. Although Darwin professed ignorance about the causes of variations, he laid emphasis on direct and definite action of external conditions and chance as two important factors of variations. Lamarck's theory boldly starts from the consideration that animals chose, by an assertion of the will, to conduct their lives in a certain manner. According to Darwin the main cause of variation is the direct action of changed conditions of existence, while with Lamarck the action of the conditions of existence is indirect, the direct action being that of the animals themselves, in consequence of changed sense of need under changed conditions. Lamarck does not attribute to the physical environment any direct transforming action on the form of species but recognises in the living being the power of varying according to needs. Lamarck's theory is not deterministic and mechanistic like Darwin's. On the other hand, Lamarck did not formulate a complete and perfect system. His theory is not adequate enough to account for the evolution of the superman.

The difference between Lamarck's approach and Butler's approach is not of kind but of degree. According to both, purpose, will, effort and heredity are the indispensable conditions that operate in the evolution of species. Bulter's concept of heredity is different from that of Lamarck, Lamarck emphasises the effect of environment which is inherited and passed on to the next generation but he does not link on the experiences of the race to that of the individual. He held that life originated from dead matter by a process of spontaneous generation while Butler looked upon the so-called inorganic world as living up to a certain point. Shaw has championed both Lamarck and Butler. But it was in the work of the latter that he found the basic clue to his doctrine of Creative Evolution.

Shaw is a staunch supporter of Creative Evolution. The idea of Creative Evolution is referred to here and there in his early writings. But it was in the dream episode in Act III of *Man and Superman* that he makes a conscious and consistent statement. The Devil says about Nietzsche:

> Well, he came here first, before he recovered his wits. I had some hopes of him; but he was a confirmed Life-Force worshipper. It was he who raked up the Superman, who is as old as Prometheus; and the 10th century will run after this newest of the old crazes when it gets tired of the world, the flesh, and your humble servant.[1]

The Statue then remaks:

> Superman is a good cry; and a good cry is half the battle. I should like to see this Nietzsche.[2]

The third Act of *Man and Superman* along with *A Revolutionist's Handbook* confirms the essence of Shaw's philosophy of the superman. Don Juan, who is Shaw's spokesman, covers that happiness does not count in life. He is bored with his life in hell, the home of the unreal and the seekers of happiness. Life is the only truth in his view and proclaims that his purpose of going to Heaven, the home of the masters of reality, is to escape from the vulgar pursuit of happiness.

It is interesting here to note that Shaw lost his faith in Christianity and renounced God early in his life and yet he is a deeply religious man. Shaw's God is Life-Force which can create a superman. The Life-Force, says Don Juan in *Man and Superman*, is the creative power behind the creation of the superman. The progressive growth of species from amoebe to man is progress. The Life-Force has purpose but its ultimate purpose is quite unknown. It seems that Life-Force has a passion for social engineering and it creates only to satisfy this urge and its creations are different stages rather than final achievements. Man is superior to all species so far evolved by the Life-Force. But the fact remains that man is not the last stage in the process of evolution. Evolution is creative.

1. *Man and Superman*, *op. cit.*, p. 172.
2. *Ibid.*

Shaw's Life-Force is not a particular sect of religion
of the term. He looks upon woman as life incarnat
man for the sole purpose of her own impregnation b
process of procreation is more economical than a sin
the woman who takes the initiative in the process of
attempt to pursue a man by a woman in *Man and S*
the gist of comedy but it also brings to focus the ph
gives a particular status to woman in the process o
super race. Her predominant function is to produc
to preserve it. Her death will be the sign of unive
purpose of her life is to carry out her mission. Tan

> It is the self-sacrificing woman that sacri
> recklessly. Because they are unselfish, the
> things. Because they have a purpose whic
> purpose, but that of the whole universe, a
> them but an instrument of that purpose.[1]

Motherhood is a life long cherished desire
natural that she will not let her purpose go in v
mere heroine of a facial comedy, for she is inc
but accomplishment of the purpose of the Life
men and women should cooperate to bring in
submitting to the purpose of Ann, Tanner bec
because, therefore, he becomes an instrume
future of the race. Ann and Tanner both embr
both dedicate themselves to a purpose whic
but of the whole universe.

The philosopher is something more th
purpose. Woman is the embodiment of Life
symbolises its intellectual consciousness; v
life while the philosopher attaches value t
species while the man of genius impro
something better by pointing out the direc
that Shaw passes a censure against Chris
view that we are not in the hands of God
must try to evolve into superman and a
evolution.

1. *Ibid.*, p. 61.

The Philanderer was written when there was hot discussion and craze for Ibsen throughout Europe. Shaw first entered the field of literature as a champion of Ibsen and not as a dramatist. Still there are basic differences between Shaw and Ibsen. Ibsen is an individualist criticising social institutions so far as they hamper social growth. Shaw is a socialist with a whip in his hand to bring socialism. But there are many similarities between the ideas of the two. Both of them are believers in revolution, though it is different in the case of each. Love to Shaw is tyranny requiring special safeguard. Sexual relationship being a biological demand needs no glorification or idealisation. Shaw attacks romantic love both in *Candida* and *Arms and the Man*. Candida's love for Marchbank is the love of calf and cow. Raina's love for Bluntschli also has very little of idealism about it. The essential function of marriage, Shaw thinks, is the continuation of the human race. His view on sex is anti-romantic.

As a great evolutionist Shaw looks at the evolution of the human race from an unconventional angle. The right of bearing a child is the most sacred right of a woman. Most women feel that motherhood is an experience necessary to their psychaic development and understanding of themselves. Shaw's ultimate objection to the institution of marriage is that it hinders creative evolution. If the superman is to come, he must be born of a woman by man's intention and well considered contrivance. Shaw invites his readers' attention to the fact that marriage fails to unite two souls. He anticipates the objection of conventionalists and counters it by showing that even the happiest of marriages is really empty of substance and what seems to be a successful alliance is really based on a pious fraud. This is reflected in Candida's character. The few incidents of married life described in *Candida* reflect that the intimate relationship between husband and wife is neither intimate nor personal. Candida and her husband Morell have hardly anything in common.

Shaw attacks conventional love and domestic happiness from another angle. Morell, the moralist, himself violates the rules of conventional morality. He appears to be truthful in his love for Candida. But he himself has an affair with Miss Proxy, his private Secretary. He is a worthy man, slightly pigheaded, and a windbag of morality, only because he is united to Candida by the institution of marriage. Judged by a conventional standard the marriage of Candida and Morell is a successful one. But its foundations rest on fraud which has been made sacred by convention. Morell is neither a tyrant nor an exploiter, yet he fails to be a good husband. Shaw's main purpose is to show that even an ideal husband is no better than a tyrant. *Candida* exposed the myth of marital harmony and domestic happiness. In *Candida*, Shaw exposes the unreality of the so-called marital love. It requires the meddling of a fantastic poet like Marchbank to show that respectable Morell is only a parasitical windbag and in electing to stay with him, the peerless Candida selects the weaker of the two and chooses the life of vulgar domesticity. Shaw says in the collection of prefaces "There is no shrinking in it. If marriage cannot be made to produce something better than we are, marriage will have to go or the nation will have to go."[1] Besides an early divorce, Shaw recommends occasional change of partner and transient casual adventures outdoors without breaking home life. Shaw appears to think that when women achieve political life, marriage will have to starve.

Marx's *Das Capital* opened Shaw's eyes to the fact that capitalism upsets the social balance in every walk of life. Sidney Trefuses, a character of *An Intelligent Woman's Guide to Socialism* says, "All rotten to the bone civilization! civilization, civilization."[2] Shaw says about capitalism in his *An Intelligent Woman's Guide to Socialism* "... it is a disease and the sins it has let loose and glorified are the seven deadly ones."[3] Shaw seems to suggest that capitalism is so all-pervasive that even the royal veto which has long gone out of use might be invoked as a bulwark against it. In Shaw's formulation of ideas the economic factors play a significant role in society. He held the view that poverty is a public nuisance and its toleration is a crime. Sartorius in *Widowers' Houses* says:

> My dear friend: these poor people do not know how to live in proper dwellings: they would wreck them in a week. You doubt me; try it for yourself. You are welcome to replace all the missing banisters, and handrails, cistern lids and dusthole tops at your own expense; and you will find them missing again in less than three days: burnt, sir, every stick of them. I do not blame the poor creatures: they need fires, and often have no other way of getting them. But I really cannot spend pound after pound in repairs for them to pull down, when I can barely get them to pay me four and six pence a week for a room, which is recognized fair London rent. No, gentlemen:

1. G.B. Shaw: *Prefaces*, Pelican Books Ltd., Australia, 1970, p. 17.
2. *Shaw the Philosopher*, op. cit., p. 70.
3. *Ibid.*

> when people are very poor, you cannot help them, no matter how much you may sympathize with them. It does them more harm than good in the long run. I prefer to save my money in order to provide additional houses for the homeless,....[1]

Instead of helping the poor, poverty should be eliminated by overthrowing capitalism.

Mrs. Warren's Profession is a political thesis in the form of a play and the uproar evoked in England by it was not without reason. It is a convincing presentation of the economic causes of prostitution. In a capitalistic society, the penalty of virtue is starvation, disease and premature death and the reward of immediate vice is relief. If, therefore, women prefer the wages of sin to the wages of manual labour it is but natural. Shaw discusses individual blackguardism, but he lays stress on the root of the malady. Mrs. Warren is an organiser of prostitution, owning and managing brothels in many countries. With this income, she has given a sound education to her daughter Vivie. When Vivie discovers the source of her mother's income, she freexes into an iceburg of contempt. It is clear that it is capitalism which has imposed prostitution not only on women but also on many classes of men—doctors, lawyers, politicians, journalists and clergymen. Shaw pricks the double by saying that doctors have vested interest in anti-social activities. In Doctor's Dilemma he considers a poor doctor more dangerous than a poor man. A devotee of Life-Force, Shaw confessed his belief in the vital force of man. Death from disease is, to Shaw, unnatural. He throws the responsibility of diseases, illness and premature death on capitalistic civilization. Duffin says:

> Poor people are cancer's in the commonwealth, costing far more than if they were handsomely pensioned off as incurables.[2]

Shaw's panacea for all diseases is socialism. By socialism he means unconditional equality of income of every body without regard to character, age, sex or property. In *Widowers' Houses* Trench says:

> Well, people who live in glass houses have no right to throw stones. But, on my honour, I never knew that my house was a glass one until you pointed it out. I beg your pardon.[3]

1. G.B. Shaw; *Plays Unpleasant, op. cit.*, p. 71.
2. Quoted by H.C. Duffin: *The Quintessence of Bernard Shaw, op. cit.*, p. 106.
3. G.B. Shaw: *Plays Unpleasant, op. cit.*, p. 73.

In his capacity as a dramatist, Shaw built not on human heart but on his thesis of economy. Shaw himself wrote in a letter to Professor Henderson: "In all my plays my economic studies have played as important a part as knowledge of anatomy does in the works of Michael Angelo."[1]

Shaw has nothing to do with an art which does not concern itself with the uplift of human beings by changing material conditions. He had contempt for the man who regards art as a quaint and costly ring in the nose of nature. To him art should first and foremost deliver the goods as nature does. Art, Shaw has asserted, is the living world of man delivering a message to his own time. Blanche says:

> Oh, I hate the poor. At least, I hate those dirty, drunken, disreputable people who live like pigs. If they must be provided for, let other people look after them. How can you expect any one to think well of us when such things are written about us in that infamous book?[2]

In *The Widowers' Houses* Shaw discusses the idea of social justice because the lack of justice makes an obstacle in the evolution of the human race, and finally it creates a blocking stone in the birth of superman. Blanche who is an intellectual character of the play, refuses to marry him because the purpose of marriage will be defeated, Dr. Trench wishes to treat Blanche like a doll in his hand but she craves for self-independence. She is not ready to surrender herself to him who cannot meet the demand of her life. Blanche says:

> 'I do not want marry a fool.'[3]

He lacks the sense of justice and insight and these two factors are responsible for the act of denial of marriage. The lack of insight and sense of justice hampers the growth of superman. Blanche unlike other Shavian characters, refuses to marry and prefers to live in widower's house because marriage with a fool will neither serve the purpose of marriage nor will it meet the biological needs. Shaw attacks the institution of marriage because society has developed it but has not made modification in it.

---

1. Quoted by Ervine St. John in *Bernnard Shaw. His Life, Works and Friends, op. cit.*, p. 136.
2. *Plays Unpleasant*, op. cit., p. 86.
3. *Ibid.*, p. 76.

Shaw also hints at the rule of sympathy because it also creates a kind of obstacle in the evolution of the race. Evolution is possible through suffering which purges the soul of a man's life. A radical change can be made only through suffering. Sartorious says:

> My young friend: when people are very poor, you can help them, no matter how much you may sympathise with them. It does them more harm than good in the long run. I prefer to save my money in order to provide additional houses for the homeless.[1]

Shaw's plays turn generally around problems of marriage. *The Widowers' Houses* deals with marriage as the right vehicle for producing better persons in society. Blanche refuses to marry Dr. Trench on the ground that he will never serve the purpose of Life-Force. He hates the system of marriage which has been outdone by the society and no change has been brought. Shaw is preoccupied with the problems of marriage because it is the most suitable vehicle which helps in producing better race. Blanche breaks up the match because it is neither congenial nor fruitful for the arrival of the superman. No doubt, Shaw wants to bring some radical changes in the institution of marriage but the fact does remain that in his play *Getting Married* and *The Widowers' Houses*, he wishes to flush out the evils in the system of marriage because it fails to help to bring any solution to the problem of the modern life:

> Blanche refuses to accept him as her husband on the presumption that Dr. Trench lacks the sense of equality.[2]

Blanche turns down the proposal of marriage keeping in view the irrationality of Dr. Trench. In *Arms and the Man* he attacks die institution of war and romance. He attacks the institution of marriage also because he had no trust in the modern system of marriage. His philosophy changes according to the need of situation. He is obsessed with the problem of marriage and sex because sex is the vehicle of creation while marriage if modified is the meeting ground of a male and a female, for procreation.

Shaw attacks the institution of marriage time and again in *Arms and the Man* because it fails to unite die intellectually male and female on equal terms at the service of life. Harmony is one of the indispensable forces

1. *Ibid.*, p. 71.
2. *Ibid.*, p. 77.

forces responsible for the procreation of superman. His concept of superman is not an original one but the fact does remain this shapes the structure and destiny of a different kinds of superman. It is a fact that Nietzsche's concept of superman and Plato's New Man made a great impact on him but the beauty of his approach lies in remodeling of the concept of superman. Raina in the early part of *Arms and the Man* does not surrender to the romantic fool Sergius because he will prove irrelevant to conjugal life. Shaw's attack on the instiuation of the marriage is mainly on account of failure to bring about no modification in it. In *The Widowers Houses* he aims at demonstrating the failure of marriage because it does not suit conditions of modern life. Conventional people marry while the more aware people dislike it. It creates a kind of obstacle in the procreation of superman. In changing contexts, the basic requirement of the modern time is modification in the institution of marriage. Blanche is against the institution of marriage and she is also against the tyranny of the husbands. What constitutes the heart of marriage is neither money nor respectability but love. Love is the core of the institution of marriage. Shaw indirectly suggests dial sex is not the right vehicle for the procreation of superman. The birth of superman requires a complete harmony between a male and a female. Blanche is against marriage which is made without any acquaintance between a male and a female. Shaw's emphasis on the selection of breeding is mainly on account of proper functioning of the Life-Force. The lack of harmony between a male and a female will naturally create an obstacle in the working of Life-Force. Blanche, like Miss Vivie of *Mrs. Warren's Profession*, does not agree to the idea of her parents because she is confident that her marriage with such a romantic idiot will fail to serve the meaning of marriage. Shaw s attack on the institution of marriage is in the interest of a radical reformation in the system of marriage. In the interest of the basic facts, common human sentiments to the sympathy or compassion are irrelevant.

> My young friend: these poor people do not know how to live in proper dwelling. They would wreck them in a week. You doubt me: Try it for yourself... When people are very poor, you cannot help them no matter how much you may sympathize with them, it does more harm than good in the long run.[1]

1. *Ibid.*, p. 71.

Shaw's language is satirical and he makes some sort of comments for making modification in the system. Society has outgrown the system but has added nothing to it which can keep the system working. Change is the second name of life. As Sartorius says in *The Widowers' Houses*:

> We live in a progressive age and humanitarian ideas are advancing and must be taken into account. But my practice is the same as his. I should hardly feel justified in making a large claim for compensation under existing circumstances.[1]

Shaw's belief in new ideas is the result of his association with the concept of superman. Idea can alone bring a change and can impress on the male and female. In the absence of innovation of new idea, nothing new can turn out. Blanche's refusal of marriage with Trench is mainly because Blanche is the girl of her times while her lover Trench still belongs to the past. Her father tries to materialise the marriage but Blanche clarities that her marriage with such fool will serve no purpose of marriage. In *Mrs. Warren's Profession*, he wants to hint that prostitution is the product of illegal system of distribution of money. A woman is not born as a quean but society enables her to lead the life of a harlot. Superman can be procreated in the conjugal harmony of male and female. The struggle between the male and female makes a greater impact on the psychic development of a child. The relation between husband and wife counts much and it makes a great effect on the psychic development and the personality of the child. But in the ecology of socialism, Candida does not yield to Marchbank because she knows that he is an innocent fool and he can never meet the needs of her life. A perfect harmony between an intellectual male and female is required for the birth of happy and developed race. Shaw emphasises that an ignorant man combined with an ignorant woman can hardly produce a better man. Ignorance is poison between a male and a female and obstructs the growth of the superman. Like Plato, Shaw insists on 'reason' which is incomparably the most important, for it partakes of the eternal; it is the most divine in a man; whereas courage and desire belong entirely to the world of time and space. It is reason, therefore, which sees the truth and directs the activity of the good soul. It is reason which is the 'The Inward Man'; the rational element in us that is our real personality. Shaw refuses to insist on the role

1. *Ibid.*, p. 89.

of courage which can be seen in the character of Napoleon. Napoleon is the man of destiny and is guided not by courage alone but by will. Shaw argues that courage is obedient to the dictates of reason and helps in the evolutionary process. Shaw considers the will of a man subordinate to human reason. Desire is strong, wilful, contentious turbulent and chaotic. Desire is constantly in arms against reason. Reason predominates over courage and desire. Blanche is guided by reason like Raina, Candida, and Miss Vivie. Courage is a factor which helps in the evolutionary process, although it is the servant of reason. It acts according to the dictates of reason.

Shaw's wise characters act according to the dictates of wisdom. Allardyce Nicoll rightly says in *World Drama:*

> His characters are not living beings with the conclusion that because of this dramatic artistry is of a sort not destined to endure. The truth of the observation may be accepted without endorsement of the conclusion. We may agree that in the whole range Shavian Drama there are not characters who assume such breathing vitality as we find in the persons of Sophocles or of Shakespeare; but that is because Shaw's approach to his characters is of a different kind. His theatre might well be described as the theatre of ideas, not in the sense that a single thought is imposed Brieux-wise, on the entire action, but rather in the sense that Shaw presents the supreme and well-nigh unique power of making the most diverse ideas take on human resemblance. His characters are the embodiments of intellectual concepts; his Drama are ceaseless dances of thought.

Shaw's characters are the embodiments of his own thought. He wishes strongly to uproot the system of marriage because marriage before a priest does not constitute the heart of marriage. Love is the cementing force of marriage. Marriage means 'to make merriment', not a purposeful biological alliance between a male and a female. In *The Widowers' Houses* Shaw pleads that conventional people like to marry while wise people make charming friendship. Shaw gives greater value to friendship because it hardly creates bitterness between a male and a female. Shaw, like Ibsen, dislikes the modern institutions of marriage because it is futile in the evolutionary process. Shaw, like Ibsen, gives greater importance to eugenics because it will lead to the birth of superman. In *Arms and the Man*, Shaw demonstrates his hatred of war and romance of human values. He attacks brutality, like D.H. Lawrence, the institution of war and marriage because both war and marriage are the embodiments of lost virtues of the human life. Bluntschli craves to escape from the net of marriage but the Life-Force does not let him escape. He becomes a tool in the grip of Life-Force. He surrenders to Raina not because of marriage but on account of Life-Force. Life-Force enables him to be engripped in the institution of marriage. He does not yield to the institution of marriage but he yields to Life-Force. Shaw attaches more importance to Life-Force because it is the embodiment of creation, more dominating in a female in comparison to a male, and that is the metaphysics behind Shavian female characters who run after the male. Even in *The Widower's Houses* the heroine is running after the hero and thus Shaw proves that the female is the runner propelled by Life-Force and the male is being chased down. Ibsen desired to break the unity of family life in his play *A Doll's House*. He has explored the exploitation of wives by husbands in the system of marriage. Nora is not satisfied with her marriage because her marriage with Helmer is a kind of exploitation of her life. In *Candida* Shaw explores the possibility of exploitation in the system of marriage but, unlike Ibsen, he does not wish to spoil the integrity and harmony of marriage. This does not mean that he does not attack the institution of marriage. Candida's marriage with Morell is a social bond and no longer a marriage. Shaw, like Jonathan Swift, speaks with his tongue in his cheeks. He does not smile at the institution of marriage but he mocks at the wrong values associated with it.

His emergence as a dramatist in the early twentieth century was the primary need of the hour. He emerged not as a propagandist, rather he emerged to wage war against the rotten ethical norms and to plead for bringing some modification in the system of marriage in order to purge marriage of its distortions. His doctrine of Life-Force is a rational equivalent to the Blood mysticism of D.H. Lawrence. The structure of the destiny of the superman is basically conceived, not preordained, but it is shaped at the conjugal moment. An accidental child cannot be a better man. Shaw, like Shakespeare, poses the question of human identity in his *Arm and the Man* on the plea that the destiny of the superman is at the cross-road. The man says in *Arms and the Man*:

> Sleep, Sleep, Sleep, Sleep, Sleep—(The words trail off into a murmur. He makes again at the shock of foiling) where am I? That is what I want to know: Where am I?[1]

Shaw's question is the question of a matured thinker who desires to transform the world into paradise but for this he does not knock at the temple of God, because man, according to Shaw, is the maker of his own destiny. Will power alone can bring about an evolution of man into superman. His supermen are no longer the solution of the topical problems of humanity, rather they are bored with their lives. His supermen and superwomen hardly pine for the improvement of their children because they take their births from eggs. Caesar, Napoleon and Androcles are no longer the samples of Superman because they are casual supermen. Bluntschli does not pose as a heroic man but he has some heroic qualities.

Evolution of man into superman is not a material process but is chiefly ideal and intellectual process. A tug of war on the philosophical front is no longer between mechanical evolution and emergent evolution. Bergson's creative evolution is also a kind of emergent evolution because there lurks in his doctrine of creativity the ideas of surprise, uncertainty. Sri Aurobindo champions the cause of emergent evolution, which constitutes a far greater role. According to the *Purusa Sukta* of the *Rig Veda*, the evolution of the world can alone be through successive emergences of higher and higher consciousness. For Sri Aurobindo, evolution does not mean merely addition of some new principle to those which are emergent. Evolution is the backbone of Sri Aurobindo's and Shaw s philosophy. Shaw has acknowledged the cosmic view of evolution of the west but has rejected its mechanical character and has replaced it by a spiritual evolution. Shaw's philosophy is neither an obstruction of the mere intellectual extension and justification of the ignorance of the human mind. There is in his gospel an integral spiritual vision, a synthetic and broad view, the rare and sublime amalgam of the ideals and approaches of the east and the west.

1. *The Complete Bernard Shaw's Plays*, year 1965, p. 100.

Sri Aurobindo does not accept that man is the last word in the process of evolution. He asserts with a greater emphasis that the final fruition of all human progress would consist in a unique form of self-exceeding and self-transcending Man as essentially a mental being. Supermanhood implies the bringing into play of the supermind in man. The superman or divine man is thus man transfigured in all the members of his being by the sovereign dynamism of spirit. The vision of the superman brings to a focus the loftiest ideals which have been inspiring mankind. It is the cause of perfection of the race and flowering of the divine in man. The superman is inevitably the playmate of the divine in his cosmic self-expressions and creative adventures. Shaw's superman is not as Nietzsche thinks him to be the highest embodiment of the biological forces of nature, not even as modified and reformed that the birth of divine in man is the supreme consummation towards which the march of human civilization has been moving through the ages.

Shaw considered his prefaces as important part of his plays. Shaw's views on politics and religion, on dictatorship and revolution, on marriage and divorce, penal reform and capital punishment, blood-sports, vivisection, education, stage censorship, medical morality and the future of private practice complicates the mind of the philosopher and leads to the cause and condition of evolution of man into superman. Shaw asserts that the evolution of man into superman is not a difficult game to be achieved but it requires a rigorous discipline on the self and rigorous command over will-power.

III

The Tree

It is in the third part of *Back to Methuselah* that we encounter the first superman which the evolutionary process has produced. It is the year 1270 A.D. and the scene is laid in the office of Burge-Lubin, the President of the British Islands. Science has made man's life easy and people retire at the age of fortythree. Time and space have been at least partly conquered and Burge-Lubin, who has apparently nothing to do in the name of administration except flirting with his Minister of Health, a beautiful negress, makes full use of it for his romantic engagements. The Archbishop of York is announced. He is a middle aged man, looking no more than fifty, but it becomes clear, after a short investigation, that he is three hundred years old. Since the official age is only seventyeight, the Archbishop has deceived the government several times by pretending to have been drowned, but it transpires that he has, in one life, led five lives, as Archbishop Haslam, Archbishop Stickit, President Dickenson, General Bullyboy and finally, the Archbishop of York. It is neither respectable, nor perhaps safe, to live for more than seventy years and the Archbishop has tried to escape the scandal that is bound to be associated with the longevity that he has been enjoying. As a matter of tact he has had to suffer a lot because of his longevity. He tells the President and the two high officials the difficulties he had to face:

> Mr. President,... I was over eighty before the 1969 Act for the Redistribution of Income entitled me to a handsome retiring pension. Owing to my youthful appearance I was persecuted for attempting to obtain public money on false pretences when I claimed it. I could prove nothing; for the register of my birth had been blown to pieces by a bomb dropped on a village church years before in the first of the modern big wars. I was ordered back to work as a man of forty, and had

> to work for fifteen years more, the retiring age then being fiftyfive....They made difficulties about letting me go even then, I still looked so young. For some years I was in continual trouble. The industrial police rounded me up again and again, refusing to believe that I was over age. They began to call me The Wandering Jew. You see how impossible my position was. I foresaw that in twenty years my official record would prove me to be seventyfive; my appearance would make It impossible to believe that I was more than forty-five; and my real age would be one hundred and seventeen. What was I to do? Bleach my hair? Hobble about on two sticks? Minic the voice of a centurian? Better have killed myself... I did kill myself. It was quite easy. I left a suit of clothes by the sea-shore during the bathing season, with documents in the pockets to identify me. I then turned up in a strange place, pretending that I had lost my memory, and did not know my name and my age of anything about myself. Under treatment I recovered my health, but not my memory. I have had several careers since I began this routine of life and death. I have been an archbishop three times. When I persuaded the authorities to knock down all our towns and rebuild them from the foundations, or move them, I went into the artillery and became a general. I have been a President.[1]

But the Archbishop is not the only man to attain this long life. Because of the process of creative evolution several persons have attained the age of three hundred years, but they have been concealing the fact from all others because they do not want to become the victims of public incredulity. A little later the Domestic Minister of the British Islands comes into the room. He looks at the Archbishop rather curiously, and after some time discloses the fact that she also is of the same age as that of the archbishop. She is in her two hundred and seventyfith year but she does not look more than forty. There is, moreover, a grace in her movements which can hypnotise a young man of thirty into asking her to marry him. This is how she looks when she enters the room:

> She is handsome woman, apparently in the prime of life, with elegant, tense, well held up figure, and the walk of a goddess.

1. G.B. Shaw: *Backk to Methuselah, op. cit.*, pp. 110-111.

> Her expression and deportment are grave, swift, decisive, awful, answerable.[1]

Outwardly she has not changed much except that there is an air of mystery in her deportment. But inwardly she has undergone a change. One of expressions of this change in her character can be seen in her attitude towards other people. Though she is only a minister, she does not show the President the respect he deserves and her behaviour towards him is marked by the condescension which a grown up person shows towards an intelligent child. She has had to take recourse to duplicity in order to hide her age, but she has gathered the wisdom which the experience of three centuries of life brings. Bernard Shaw, in the later parts of the pentateuch, emphasises this aspect of the change in the personality of the superman. Age brings them a deeper insight into things, and their attitude towards each other is determined by the change that has taken place in their temperament and character. Naturally the supermen of the last books of the pentateuch are not the kind of supermen that were to serve as Cain's ideal; they are more philosophers who are interested in seeking the answer to the question of the purpose of human existence than power-seekers who aspire to rule over and control the destiny of others.

The Archbishop tells the President and his short-lived friends that he regards them to be no more than children though he has all along been forced by circumstances to hide his real feelings towards them and to show them the deference that their position demands. He says:

> Can you short-lived people not understand that as the confusion and immaturity and primitive animalism in which we live for first hundred years of our life is worse in this matter of sex than in any other, you are intolerable to us in that relation.[2]

When Burge-Lubin asks the Archbishop and Mrs. Lutestrong if they regard him as a mere child, Mrs. Lutestrong replies:

> Do you expect me to regard you as a completed soul? Oh, you may well be afraid of me. There are moments when your levity, your ingratitude, your shallow jollity, make my gorge

1. *Ibid.*, p. 113.
2. *Ibid.*, p. 122.

> rise so against you that if I could not remind myself that you are a child I should be tempted to doubt your right to life at all.

The Archbishop and Mrs. Lutestrong decide to marry each other because they have many things in common and leave the office of the President. The Secretary of the government tells those that are present in the room that the consequences of a long life are going to be disastrous for the community. Everything that is held sacred today will lose importance in the eyes of the people and unpleasant things which make people shudder even to think of will happen:

> "Things will happen which you do not foresee: terrible things. The family will dissolve; parents and children will be no longer the old and young; brothers and sisters will meet as strangers after a hundred years separation; the ties of blood will lose their innocence. The imagination of men, let loose over the possibilities of three centuries of life, will drive them mad and wreck human society."

Confusius, the secretary, has really seen the future and what he has foretold does come to pass in *Tragedy of an Elderly Gentleman* and *As Far as Thought can Reach*. In *Tragedy of an Elderly Gentleman*, we are given a picture of life at a place in Ireland of 30000 A.D. The world is now inhabited by supermen and also shortlivers who live for less than one hundred years. The supermen have taken control of things in every walk of life and it is not with condescension but with disgust that they look at the shortlivers. They are now the normal race and since the shortlivers are freaks and mentally and physically handicapped people, a thorough campaign goes on to eliminate them. The result is that a shortliver child is killed in childhood itself when it becomes clear that he or she is a shortliver. The family has dissolved almost completely and the ties of blood have lost their innocence. It is a grim world though a grimmer one is yet to appear in the last part of the play—and the things which are apparently funny have really an undercurrent horror.

An elderly gentleman, a shortliver, sits alone on the seashore, apparently unhappy because he finds that he does not understand many things at the place. He is a foreigner and is unacquainted with the new culture which has emerged at the island where the duration of life has risen to about one thousand years. He begins sobbing because he is overwhelmed by the feeling of loneliness. Immediately after a woman appears there. "Her age cannot be guessed: her face is firm and chiselled like a young face; but her expression is unyouthful in its severity and determination."[1]

The woman examines him and diagnoses his disease as being the disease of discouragement. This discouragement is in reality extreme pessimism caused by the inability to adjust to the new state of things. This is a disease which the new race does not suffer from. This new race has eliminated a large number of words from the dictionary because they are no longer required. Some such words are lady doctor, decency, tresspassing, sneer, embarrassment, blush, civilization, nap, sleep, pauper and shilling. It is clear that in this new society physical ailments do not exist, social norms of behaviour have been done away with, the difference between the public and the private no longer exists, humour is dead, and currency is no longer in currency. They have done away with most material things because they do not need them; evidently they do not need even food or sleep. People are called by the name of Zoo and Zozim; they have no surnames whatsoever because the family has dissolved, and the meanings of the proper names do not count since they are intended only to differentiate one individual from another.

It is a society in which, as Zoo informs the elderly gentleman, there are only two human classes: "the short-lived and the normal. The normal people are divided into primaries, secondaries and tertiaries—those in their first century, those in their second century, and those in their third century. They are valued in accordance with seniority in age since these people have no families, babies are allowed to be born only to those females that are mentally and physically fit for the purpose. If a woman is really good, she is allowed to specialise in producing babies. Mothers are not interested in their children after the latter have attained the age of ten.

Zoo, one of the major characters of *Tragedy of an Elderly Gentleman*, who is also a longliver, a superman, tells the elderly gentleman, "It is a law of nature that there is a fixed relation between conduct and length of life."[2] She is evidently speaking for her creator himself because in the play we find that the character of the supermen and superwomen has been changed by the fact that they have acquired long lives. Their laws

1. *Ibid.*, p. 139.
2. *Ibid.*, p. 171.

overwhelmed by the feeling of loneliness. Immediately after a woman appears there. "Her age cannot be guessed: her face is firm and chiselled like a young face; but her expression is unyouthful in its severity and determination."[1]

The woman examines him and diagnoses his disease as being the disease of discouragement. This discouragement is in reality extreme pessimism caused by the inability to adjust to the new state of things. This is a disease which the new race does not suffer from. This new race has eliminated a large number of words from the dictionary because they are no longer required. Some such words are lady doctor, decency, tresspassing, sneer, embarrassment, blush, civilization, nap, sleep, pauper and shilling. It is clear that in this new society physical ailments do not exist, social norms of behaviour have been done away with, the difference between the public and the private no longer exists, humour is dead, and currency is no longer in currency. They have done away with most material things because they do not need them; evidently they do not need even food or sleep. People are called by the name of Zoo and Zozim; they have no surnames whatsoever because the family has dissolved, and the meanings of the proper names do not count since they are intended only to differentiate one individual from another.

It is a society in which, as Zoo informs the elderly gentleman, there are only two human classes: "the short-lived and the normal. The normal people are divided into primaries, secondaries and tertiaries—those in their first century, those in their second century, and those in their third century. They are valued in accordance with seniority in age since these people have no families, babies are allowed to be born only to those females that are mentally and physically fit for the purpose. If a woman is really good, she is allowed to specialise in producing babies. Mothers are not interested in their children after the latter have attained the age of ten.

Zoo, one of the major characters of *Tragedy of an Elderly Gentleman*, who is also a longliver, a superman, tells the elderly gentleman, "It is a law of nature that there is a fixed relation between conduct and length of life."[2] She is evidently speaking for her creator himself because in the play we find that the character of the supermen and superwomen has been changed by the fact that they have acquired long lives. Their law

1. *Ibid.*, p. 139.
2. *Ibid.*, p. 171.

> to work for fifteen years more, the retiring age then being fiftyfive....They made difficulties about letting me go even then, I still looked so young. For some years I was in continual trouble. The industrial police rounded me up again and again, refusing to believe that I was over age. They began to call me The Wandering Jew. You see how impossible my position was. I foresaw that in twenty years my official record would prove me to be seventyfive; my appearance would make It impossible to believe that I was more than forty-five; and my real age would be one hundred and seventeen. What was I to do? Bleach my hair? Hobble about on two sticks? Minic the voice of a centurian? Better have killed myself... I did kill myself. It was quite easy. I left a suit of clothes by the sea-shore during the bathing season, with documents in the pockets to identify me. I then turned up in a strange place, pretending that I had lost my memory, and did not know my name and my age of anything about myself. Under treatment I recovered my health, but not my memory. I have had several careers since I began this routine of life and death. I have been an archbishop three times. When I persuaded the authorities to knock down all our towns and rebuild them from the foundations, or move them, I went into the artillery and became a general. I have been a President.[1]

But the Archbishop is not the only man to attain this long life. Because of the process of creative evolution several persons have attained the age of three hundred years, but they have been concealing the fact from all others because they do not want to become the victims of public incredulity. A little later the Domestic Minister of the British Islands comes into the room. He looks at the Archbishop rather curiously, and after some time discloses the fact that she also is of the same age as that of the archbishop. She is in her two hundred and seventyfith year but she does not look more than forty. There is, moreover, a grace in her movements which can hypnotise a young man of thirty into asking her to marry him. This is how she looks when she enters the room:

> She is handsome woman, apparently in the prime of life, with elegant, tense, well held up figure, and the walk of a goddess.

1. G.B. Shaw: *Backk to Methuselah, op. cit.*, pp. 110-111.

Her expression and deportment are grave, swift, decisive, awful, answerable.[1]

Outwardly she has not changed much except that there is an air of mystery in her deportment. But inwardly she has undergone a change. One of expressions of this change in her character can be seen in her attitude towards other people. Though she is only a minister, she does not show the President the respect he deserves and her behaviour towards him is marked by the condescension which a grown up person shows towards an intelligent child. She has had to take recourse to duplicity in order to hide her age, but she has gathered the wisdom which the experience of three centuries of life brings. Bernard Shaw, in the later parts of the pentateuch, emphasises this aspect of the change in the personality of the superman. Age brings them a deeper insight into things, and their attitude towards each other is determined by the change that has taken place in their temperament and character. Naturally the supermen of the last books of the pentateuch are not the kind of supermen that were to serve as Cain's ideal; they are more philosophers who are interested in seeking the answer to the question of the purpose of human existence than power-seekers who aspire to rule over and control the destiny of others.

The Archbishop tells the President and his short-lived friends that he regards them to be no more than children though he has all along been forced by circumstances to hide his real feelings towards them and to show them the deference that their position demands. He says:

> Can you short-lived people not understand that as the confusion and immaturity and primitive animalism in which we live for first hundred years of our life is worse in this matter of sex than in any other, you are intolerable to us in that relation.[2]

When Burge-Lubin asks the Archbishop and Mrs. Lutestrong if they regard him as a mere child, Mrs. Lutestrong replies:

> Do you expect me to regard you as a completed soul? Oh, you may well be afraid of me. There are moments when your levity, your ingratitude, your shallow jollity, make my gorge

1. *Ibid.*, p. 113.
2. *Ibid.*, p. 122.

> rise so against you that if I could not remind myself that you are a child I should be tempted to doubt your right to life at all.

The Archbishop and Mrs. Lutestrong decide to marry each otl because they have many things in common and leave the office of t President. The Secretary of the government tells those that are present the room that the consequences of a long life are going to be disastrous the community. Everything that is held sacred today will lose importar in the eyes of the people and unpleasant things which make peo shudder even to think of will happen:

> "Things will happen which you do not foresee: terrible things. The family will dissolve; parents and children will be no longer the old and young; brothers and sisters will meet as strangers after a hundred years separation; the ties of blood will lose their innocence. The imagination of men, let loose over the possibilities of three centuries of life, will drive them mad and wreck human society."

Confusius, the secretary, has really seen the future and what he foretold does come to pass in *Tragedy of an Elderly Gentleman* and *Far as Thought can Reach*. In *Tragedy of an Elderly Gentleman*, we given a picture of life at a place in Ireland of 30000 A.D. The world is inhabited by supermen and also shortlivers who live for less than hundred years. The supermen have taken control of things in every of life and it is not with condescension but with disgust that they lo the shortlivers. They are now the normal race and since the short are freaks and mentally and physically handicapped people, a thor campaign goes on to eliminate them. The result is that a shortliver is killed in childhood itself when it becomes clear that he or sh shortliver. The family has dissolved almost completely and the blood have lost their innocence. It is a grim world though a gr one is yet to appear in the last part of the play—and the things wh apparently funny have really an undercurrent horror.

An elderly gentleman, a shortliver, sits alone on the s apparently unhappy because he finds that he does not understar things at the place. He is a foreigner and is unacquainted with culture which has emerged at the island where the duration o risen to about one thousand years. He begins sobbing beca and values also are totally different. They do not know what blushing is, and when Zoo blushes because she has been insulted by the elderly gentleman, she loses her temper. She is unable to understand what has happened to her and she thinks that it is something evil for which the elderly gentleman deserves to be killed. She tells him angrily:

> Whatever you are doing, it is something so utterly evil that if you do not stop I will kill you.[1]

The elderly gentleman apologises for his words and says he withdraws what he has said. Zoo remarks, "How can you withdraw what you said?"

The gentleman replies,

> "I can say no more than that I am sorry."

Zoo feels a little relieved because her blushes are now subsiding. She is mollified and says, "The hideous sensation you gave me is subsiding; but you have had a very narrow escape. Do not attempt to kill me again; for at the first sign in your face and voice I shall strike you dead."[2]

As a matter of fact the longlivers kill everything which they find to be unacceptable in their scheme of things. They kill their own children when they find that they are shortlivers. Zoo suggests that all shortlivers throughout the world should be killed at the same time because they will, thereby, be saved many an awkward situation. When the elderly gentleman offers to be killed, she tells him, "It would be useless unless all the shortlivers were killed at the same time. Besides, it is a measure which should be taken politically and constitutionally, not privately."[3]

There are two political parties in her country which is inhabited by, primarily, longlivers: the Conservative Party and the Colonisation Party. The Conservative Party believes that it would be better if the longlivers confine themselves to their islands a race apart, wrapped up in the majesty of our wisdom on a soil held as holy ground for us by an adoring world, with our sacred frontier traced beyond dispute by the sea. The Colonisation Party, on the other hand believes that the longlivers should colonise the country of the shortlivers and systematically annihilate the latter so that after some time only longlivers, the normal people, are left

1. *Ibid.*, p. 168.
2. *Ibid.*
3. *Ibid.*, p. 169.

on the face of the earth. Zoo thinks that for the shortlivers "increase in years is only increase of sorrow; but for a longliver every extra year is a prospect which forces him to stretch his faculties to the utmost."[1] So the shortlivers must be exterminated in their own interest and superseded by the longlivers.

It is rather a ferocious world which is emerging before our eyes in *Tragedy of an Elderly Gentleman*. It is a world where all emotions have been dispensed with and people have begun to cherish a new kind of ideal. The supermen and superwomen live for three hundred years or more but more remarkable than their long life is the fact that longevity has changed their character fundamentally, and kindness, generosity and mercy no longer form part of it. Their pursuits now are not the same as those of people who live for one hundred years or less; risen above the needs of the body as they are, they devote themselves to the search of some greater truth which has escaped the human race. But what strikes the reader of the play is that they have, instead of growing into superhuman, become subhuman and even mechanical. The sentiments which the human heart is swayed with raise man above a beast and far above a mechanical device. The supermen and superwomen of the play, bereft of these finer sentiments, degenerate into a kind of superbeasts. One is constrained to ask oneself: Did Bernard Shaw really cherish such an ideal for mankind, or was he speaking with his tongue in the cheek?

The superman of *Tragedy of an Elderly Gentleman* have created a new civilization which is not a little removed from the human civilization we know about. Till now the march of civilization has resulted in the growth of new cities with more and more amenities, but in the new land there are no cities at all—not perhaps even villages—and people gather together only when there are social and communal functions. London is now a memory or not even that. The elderly gentleman asks Zoo to be shown the ruins of London, and she replies, "We do not tolerate ruins. Was London a place of importance?"[2]

Shaw's concept of superman which has been worked out in *Man and Superman* is reinforced in *Back to Methuselah*. His superman does not take birth in the play *Man and Superman*, but the reader is made to confront superman of several kinds, from Cain to the He-Ancients

1. *Ibid.*, p. 71.
2. *Ibid.*, p. 174.

and She-Ancients in *Back to Methuselah*. His theory of the Life-Force is neither overshadowed by intellect nor is it attached with the mysticism of D.H. Lawrence who conceives sex as a mystical experience. Unlike the sex theory of D.H. Lawrence and the theory of personal relationship of E.M. Forster, Shaw's Life-Force works through the help of a couple, comprising of a male and female. Male is the game and female is the hunter. Ann in *Man and Superman* is running after Tanner to marry him but Tanner does not desire to be wedded because he does not consider himself fit to procreate the superman. Shaw emphasises the moral value which helps in the evolution of the super race. Tanner says to Ann:

> Are you sure it was not that we were beginning to be something more? What does the beginning of manhood and womanhood mean in most people's mouths? You know: it means the beginning of love. But love began long before that for me. Love played its part in the earliest dreams and follies and romances I can remember—may I say the earliest follies and romances we can remember? though we did not understand it at the time. No : the change that came to me was the birth in me of moral passion; and I declare that according to my experience moral passion is the only real passion.[1]

Shaw emphasises the point that the birth of superman requires a moral growth in the people. He also stresses the point that man's guiding force is wisdom and not appetite. Wisdom is not communicable to everybody and it is an important factor which helps in the birth of the superman. Tanner and Ann are guided by reason and not by emotion because emotions will complicate sexual relationship aimed at the procreation of superman. Ann's ruling factor of life is wisdom and it is evident in her remarks on different issues. For instance, she knows well why some men refuse to marry for quite some time:

> Yes, I know. All the same, Jack, men like that always live in comfortable bachelor lodgings with broken hearts, and are adored by their landladies, and never get married. Men like you always get married.[2]

---

1. G.B. Shaw: *Man and Superman, op. cit.*, p. 73.
2. *Ibid.*, p. 204.

Tanner succumbs to Ann's plan not because he is blind to it but because he finds himself powerless:

> It is false. I love you. The Life-Force enchants me. I have the whole world in my arms when I clasp you. But I am fighting for my freedom, for my honour, for my self, one and indivisible.[1]

Tanner is not prepared to be entrapped in the net of marriage. Marriage is a soul-crushing load, and he endeavours to remain free as long as possible.

> Marriage is to me apostasy, profanation of the sanctuary of my soul, violation of my manhood, sale of my birthright, shameful surrender, ignominious capitulation, acceptance of defeat. I shall decay like a thing that has served its purpose and is done with; I shall change from a man with a future to a man with a past; I shall see in the greasy eyes of all the others husbands their relief at the arrival of a new prisoner to share their ignominy. The young men will scorn me as one who has sold out: to the women I, who have always been an enigma and a possibility, shall be merely somebody else's property—and damaged goods at that: a second-hand man at best.[2]

Shaw describes *Back to Methuselah* as a second legend of Creative Evolution. This metabiological pentateuch is not only a re-statement of the philosophy of the earlier work but also an enlargement of it. In *Man and Superman* Don Juan resolves to search out the final aim of Creative Evolution but it is the ancients in *Back to Methuselah* who have discovered this destination which is revealed as disentanglement of life from matter.

The philosophy reinforced in *Back to Methuselah* is dualistic. The two primary realities, Shaw postulates, are life and matter. Lilith's final speech is an epitome of the entire evolutionary movement. The cosmic process was set in motion when life, which was originally a whirl-pool in pure force, entered into matter. The mystery of the origin of life and the universe has never been solved and will never be solved. Theologians attempted to solve it by the method of Deux ex Machina; scientists plead that matter is behind the cause of creation. Theologians' approach and scientists' approach are no more sound and convincing than Shaw's

1. *Ibid.*, p. 205.
2. *Ibid.*, p. 203

argument. He calls upon man to make himself a vigilant agent and take the work of evolution in his own hand. In *Back to Methuselah* he explores the theme of transition according to which man's journey is too brief to be taken seriously. The consciousness of the brevity of life makes men scatter-brained, as a result of which he behaves like an irresponsible child. In the second part, he has worked out his theory of brief living. Political and social problems raised by civilization cannot be solved by men who die and decay fast. Shaw continuously voices a serious warning to humanity that if men persist in their childish follies and weaknesses Nature will try to experiment with another species. Shaw's superman will be a man of blood and flesh and will be fallible like human beings. But the fact does remain that his sole norm of guidance will be reason and not emotion. Candida and Raina do not surrender to the romantic lunatics because they know that they are hardly men of blood and flesh and in the ultimate hour, they will fail. Don Juan says rightly:

> Why not say flesh and blood at once, though we have left those two greasy commonplaces behind us?[1]

Adam in '*Back to Methuselah*' knows well that he is the son of immortality and will never be a subject of death. Eve and Adam both know full well that the destiny of their life is in their own hands because they are the captains of their own souls and they can do what they like. The serpent's advice to Eve embraces Shaw's philosophy of Creative Evolution through which the superman will be produced. Imagination is the signal of creation. We create what we imagine. We desire what we will; we will what we imagine and lastly we create what we desire. The brothers Barnabas preach that if men and women are made conscious of the fact that the will is creative, they can achieve a longer span of life by simply willing it.

Shaw's developing philosophy comes to a stop in his *Back to Methuselah*. In this play we notice him emphasizing the will which lets a man create what he desires. He does not ignore the inner force of man which serves as a help in the evolution of the superman. He fails to convince us that the ancients are improved specimens of humanity. The final stage of human evolution seems forbidding rather than alluring. He calls upon men to kiss creative evolution as their religion. The Life-Force alone can release man from his ennui by creating the superman.

1. *Ibid*., p. 171.

Even in *Man and Superman* Shaw introduces a note of warning, the Devil says:

> Ay, Rembrandt. There is something unnatural about these fellows. Do not listen to their gospel, Senor Commander: it is dangerous. Beware of the pursuit of the Superhuman: it leads to an indiscriminate contempt for the Human. To a man, horses and dogs and cats are mere species, outside the moral world. Well, to the Superman, men and women are a mere species too, also outside the moral world. This Don Juan was kind to women and courteous to men as your daughter here was kind to her pet cats and dogs; but such kindness is a denial of the exclusively human character of the soul.[1]

Shaw has worked out a new religion in *Back to Methuselah*. The new religion is a metaphysical faith in a metaphysical Life-Force, of which spiritual evolution is the outward visible sign. Shaw, after contemplating the whole of life, makes what seems to us a great imaginative leap to the hypothesis of a living will to more and more power and knowledge. To himself, it seems a simple observation of facts; to others it is not a scientific hypothesis, capable of evidence, but a religious conception, demanding faith. The truth of a religion is measured, if it can be measured at all, by its effect upon conduct, and Shaw declares that to deny purpose in the universe as new Darwinism does, is to break the skeleton of civilization. That Shaw regards Creative Evolution as something more than an explanation, is shown by his reply to a newspaper interviewer who asked him some time in 1937:

> "What is your wish for the future?" Shaw replied: "The religion of creative evolution as opposed to the mechanical theory of Darwin. What man of intellect can accept all the theisms which have been invented so far? And yet we need a God in whose name to live and work."[2]

The religious purpose of the play finds a full expression in Part V. In Part I, he shows us the starting of Creative Evolution in the discovery, on the part of life, of the twin instruments of progress—birth and death. The intermediate three parts have suggested that evolution has reached a

1. *Ibid.*, pp. 171-72.
2. Quoted by H.C. Duffin, *op. cit.*, p. 195.

stage where these two tools cannot operate any longer; another effort of will is needed to invent a third device—probably longevity. Part V shows us the new beings thus evolved—the ancients—striving to eliminate one of the earlier factors, death, by releasing life from its dependence on matter.

Evolution takes place because all life is purposeful. To Shaw evolution from within is much more genuine than evolution from outside. He calls will as the most indispensable force of creation and it is one of the potent weapons for the constitution of the superman. It is one of his beliefs that man's will can change his destiny, if his will is strong. He, therefore, suggests that man should rule over his evolution by an exertion of the will, and rise step by step in the process of evolution.

Shaw's theory of Creative Evolution is Lamarckian and Butlerian. It is Lamarckian in the sense that living organisms change because of their inner urge to change. Shaw is indebted to Butler who was in his own circle the greatest writer of the later half of the 19th century. The credit goes to Butler to enable Shaw to focus his attention on the fact that Darwin had banished his mind from the human universe. Butler and Shaw are of the same category because both of them believe that effort and will are two important factors of evolution. But the difference lies in the fact of Butler's turning down Lamarck's postulate that the effects or attempts of an individual animal during its life-time are inherited and transmitted to posterity. Butler's philosophy is monistic. He thinks that human action goes to help in the birth of the superman. The cosmic drama, according to him, started when life entered into being. Butler calls unconscious instinct, as opposed to the speculative intellect, the most encouraging factor in the scale of evolution. The fundamental point of difference of Shavian philosophy is that life evolves from a lesser to a greater degree of consciousness. The ideal individual according to him is omnipotent, omniscient and infallible. Shaw gives a very important place to women in the competition of human evolution because she is a primary tool of creation. She is the embodiment of both creation and creator. The initial form of life was a woman—Lilith—who, urged by a desire to create, tore herself into two. As the Life-Force operates through her, she is the primary runner in the evolutionary process. Shaw's doctrine of Creative Evolution is a development on Lamarck's and Butler's.

Plato has worked out the concept of the new man in his *The Republic* and according to him also the birth of the new man is possible only by selective breeding. Shaw's concept of the superman makes a total departure from Plato's concept of the new man. Plato's new man is not endowed with the powers which Shaw's superman possesses. Plato believed that it is the duty of the state to bring the best men and the best women together. Shaw believes in co-operation rather than compulsion. The best men and the best women were to be brought together through the force of Creative Evolution, and not by the dictates of the state. He also emphasises different factors needed for the existence of the superman. The basic tool of the production of the superman is a sexual encounter between intellectual male and female promoted in a social, political or economic condition affording the maximum opportunity through total freedom and equality. Shaw's superman is a creature of blood and flesh endowed with the tremendous potentialities of a God. Unlike Plato, Shaw has both propounded his theory of superman and has demonstrated it in his *Back to Methuselah*. Shaw, unlike Plato, has emphasised the power of Will which lets a man live for more than a thousand years. Plato advocated communism in sex-relationship, but Shaw accepted the institution of marriage, though not ungrudgingly as one of the tools of Life-Force. The Waiter in *You Never Can Tell says:*

> Cheer up, sir, cheer up. Every man is frightened of marriage when it comes to the point; but it often turns out very comfortable, very enjoyable and happy indeed, sir from time to time. I never was master in my own house, sir—my wife was like your young lady: she was of a commanding and masterful disposition, which my son has inherited. But if I had my life to live twice over, I'd do it again: I'd do it again, I assure you. You never can tell, sir: you never can tell.[1]

Plato, unlike Shaw, hammers on many issues, such as communism of wives, the development of education and the question of justice. His new man is guided by wisdom, while Shaw's superman is guided mainly by reason though appetite and courage are also the guiding factors of his life. Shaw's concept of superman is a refined one, while Plato's doctrine of the new man is based on imagination and utopia.

---

1. G.B. Shaw: *Complete Plays With Prefaces*, Vol. VI, Dodd, Mead & Co., New York, 1962, p. 721.

Shaw's superman is a wise man who has a profound knowledge of human behaviour and psychology. Eve and Adam are the best instance to prove it. Shaw treats sex in naked term of biology, like D.H. Lawrence and Huxley, but the fact remains that the world of mystical experience of Lawrence is similar to that of to Wordsworth and Shelley, while, on the contrary, Shaw is not mystical either in his doctrine of Life-Force or in the concept of superman. Man has got no independent entity apart from woman because it is she who creates man and the Life-Force works through her. Shaw does not idealise women in his plays because they are creatures of blood and flesh, and their basic motto is to preserve the fittest man.

Love to Shaw is a tyranny against which special safeguard is required, because it entraps a man and thus creates an obstacle in the birth of the superman. Tanner says:

> Is that any reason why you are not to call your soul your own? Oh, I protest against this vile objection of youth to age! Look at fashionable society as you know it. What does it pretend to be? An exquisite dance of nymphs. What is it? A horrible procession of wretched girls, each in the claws of a cynical, cunning, avaricious, disillusioned, ignorantly experienced, foulminded old woman whom she calls mother, and whose duty it is to corrupt her mind and sell her to the highest bidder. Why do these unhappy slaves marry anybody, however old and vile, sooner than not many at all? Because marriage is their only means of escape from these decrepit friends who hide their selfish ambitions, their jealous hatreds of the young rivals who have supplanted them, under the mask of maternal duty and family affection. Such things are abominable: the voice of nature proclaims for the daughter a father's care and for the son a mother's. The law for father and son and mother and daughter is not the law of love: it is the law of revolution, of emancipation, of final supersession of the old and worn-out by the young and capable. I tell you, the first duty of manhood and womanhood is a Declaration of Independence, the man who pleads his father's authority is no man: the woman who

> pleads her mother's authority is unfit to bear citizens to a free people.[1]

The birth of the superman requires a revolution both in the field of matrimony and patrimony. Sexual relationship being a biological demand needs no glorification or idealization. The birth of the superman has got no value and no meaning if there is disparity in the field of economics, politics and justice which are instruments in the hand of rich and powerful persons to oppress the poor and the weak. Shaw holds that the male matters nothing to the female apart from her sexual needs because he is an instrument of her purpose of creation. Don Juan says:

> Pardon me, Ana: I said nothing about a woman's whole mind. I spoke of her view of Man as a separate sex. It is no more cynical than her view of herself as above all things a Mother. Sexually, Woman is Nature's contrivance for perpetuating its highest achievement. Sexually, Man is Woman's contrivance for fulfilling Nature's behest in the most economical way. She knows by instinct that far back in the evolutional process she invented him, differentiated him, created him in order to produce something better than the single-sexed process can produce. Whilst he fulfils the purpose for which she made him, he is welcome to his dreams, his follies, his ideals, his heroisms, provided that the keystone of them all is the worship of woman, of motherhood, of the family of the hearth. But how rash and dangerous it was to invent a separate creature whose sole function was her own impregnation! For mark what has happened. First Man has multiplied on her hands until there are as many men as women; she that she has been unable to employ for her purposes more than a fraction of the immense energy she has left at his disposal by saving him the exhausting labour of gestation. This superfluous energy has gone to his brain and to his muscle. He has become too strong to be controlled by her bodily, and too imaginative and mentally vigorous to be content with mere self-reproduction. He has created civilization without consulting her, taking her domestic labour for granted as the foundation of It.[2]

1. G.B. Shaw: *Man and Superman, op. cit.*, pp. 96-97.
2. *Ibid.*, pp. 147-48.

He emphasises that the governing factor of a woman's personality is nothing but sex. He says:

> Yes, of her purpose; and that purpose is neither her happiness nor yours, but Nature's. Vitality in a woman is a blind fury of creation. She sacrifices herself to it: do you think she will hesitate to sacrifice you?[1]

Shaw suggested that woman's primary concern with being a mother shows her obsession with the Life-Force. The creation of the superman will remain an utopian concept in the absence of the Life-Force whose chief agent is woman. Shaw insists on the theory of eugenics because divorced from eugenics, his concept of superman will remain only a dream and the superman will never emerge.

Shaw's Caesar, Cleopatra and St. Joan are superpersons in the same way in which Cain in *Back to Methuselah* is a superman. Caesar is a superman who fights bravely when there is no danger. He thinks that he is more dangerous than danger itself, and this is known to danger too. Caesar has all the ingredients of a superman. He is put to death because he was prepared to embrace death. Death was also ready to kiss him. Shakespeare's Caesar is put to death because time is the most important force there and it takes him to the valley of death. Shaw's Caesar moves nearer to death because he had not the ambition to be known as a coward in the book of history. He was the maker of his own destiny. Shaw's St. Joan enjoyed life like a brave soul and she did not speak a single word of grievance against God even when she was put to torture. She fought like a brave soldier against the British intruders. She did not bother about the act of physical chastisement which she received from time to time. She is a superlady who had the courage to lead a battalion in the battle-field.

Shaw makes a complete departure from the Greek thought which held that man is a toy in the hand of destiny. Shakespeare insists on destiny and action of man, but Shaw confines his ideology mainly to will-power which constitutes and shapes the destiny of a man. Female has a greater importance in the cause of evolution of man into superman. The evolution of man into superman is a long and gradual creative process. It is not the result of accidents. The serpent in *Back to Methuselah* makes it vivid that Death is not the end of the cycle of human life but on the

---

1. *Ibid.*, p. 60.

other hand it is the migration of the soul to a new body. Shaw, like a great genius, adds a new dimension to the process in the procreation of superman. The Serpent says:

> "She told to me a marvellous story of something that never happened to Lilith that never was. She did know then that Imagination is the beginning of creation. You imagine what you desire; you will what you imagine; and at least you create what you will."[1]

Imagination is a primary stage of evolution, and it is also the cause and condition of evolution of man into superman. Imagination is always creative and it is not the product of pure fancy of the mind. He also insists on desire because it is a secondary root of evolution of man into superman. No doubt, desire is the root cause of the evolution in the social institutions. Eve's imaginative power is so mighty that she is brooding over tearing herself in order to procreate a new man. Evolution is the result of maturity and growth of the imaginative faculty. Man himself is responsible for the delay in evolution. The Serpent explores the greatness of the creative power of imagination:

> "Do Dare It. Everything is possible; everything, Listen; I am old. I am the old serpent, older than Adam, older than Eve. I remembered Lilith, who came before Adam and Eve. I was her darling as I am yours. She was alone; There was no man with her. She saw death as you saw it when the foun fell; and she knew then that she must find out to renew herself and caste the skin herself. She had a mighty will; She strove and strove and willed and willed for more moons than there are the leaves on all the trees of the garden. Her pangs were terrible: Her groans drove sleep from Eden: She said it must never be again: that the burden of remaining life was past bearing: That it was too much for one. And when she cast the skin, Lo! There was not one new Lilith but two: One like herself, the other like Adam: You were the one: Adam was the other."[2]

Shaw imparts a greater value to women because man will prove futile in absence of the companion of an intellectual lady. Harmony in

1. *The Complete Works of Bernard Shaw, 1965;* place Paul Hamlyn, London, p. 858.
2. *Ibid.* P. 858.

a conjugal life is a fundamental requisition in the creation of superman. Eve, in her debate with the serpent, puts forth a convincing argument that the decline or evolution of man mainly depends upon woman. It is she who brings a radical and creative evolution in man. Man cannot create like Lilith. The will to create is a prerequisite condition in the procreation of the superman. Shaw's philosophy of evolution of man into superman takes a turn in *Back to Methuselah.* Adams will be incapable of creating Eves without new Eves and they will die like fawn. As the Serpent says:

> They cannot renew themselves without Eves: Sooner or later you will die like the fawn; and the new Adams will be unable to create without new Eves. You can imagine such an end; but you cannot desire it, therefore cannot will it, therefore cannot create Adams only."[1]

Shaw seems to be attempting an assimilation of different heterogeneous elements which go to assist in the procreation of superman. The birth of superman is based neither on eugenics alone nor in the modification of the institution of marriage; it depends on social, political, economic and biological factors as well. He brings into play a host of factors leading to the evolution of superman. The predominance of will-power can smoothly bring about a drastic alteration in the evolution of man. He imparts different new shades of ideas because ideas alone can influence the actions of man. A man does not live in the ideological world alone. He is bound to be affected by social, historical, political and ethical norms of life. Shaw does not waver between doubt and faith, sentiment and reason. He is firm in his belief and approach. He is not so much a propagandist for his belief as an artist putting into effect his conviction that ideas can change and reorient the course of human life in line with the purpose of evolution. Ideas alone can improve the standard of creative thought and put man above narrow prejudices like caste, creed, colour which are the obstacles in the evolution of man into superman. Thought is the second name of man's life. Evolution in ideas is also one of the important ingredients which contributes to the process of procreation of superman. The Serpent says:

> I am very subtle; but man is deeper in his thought than I am. The woman knows that there is no such thing as nothing; the

1. *Ibid.*

> man knows that there is no such day as tomorrow. I do well worship them."[1]

Shaw had to remain a propagandist for some of his ideals which he cultivated in his practical life. In some of his plays he is neither a reformer nor a propagandist. In *You Never Can Tell*, he is preoccupied with moralising to the reader. It is not very difficult to prove the debt of Shaw to the tradition of revolt; the difficulty lies in his proving resistance to it. One of the first to define the new world movement, Shaw is at once a full-fledged member of this movement and one who saw it within history. He has an extraordinary revolutionary ideal of a journalist fighting for political, moral, artistic and religious reforms. Since the rebel rooted in history is doubleminded and the reforming journalist is singleminded, Shaw's two functions are not really compatible. And since Shaw's reformist propaganda is often more noisy and vehement than his dramatic art, there are times when the artistic achievements are less conspicuous than his active canvassing for utopian ideas.

Shaw's endeavour for bringing a radical change in the social system is a part of the basic demand for the evolution of a man into a superman. In *The Doctor's Dilemma* he does not simply expose social machinery but also asserts that a poor doctor is not simply fatal to the human life but a great obstacle to the evolution of the human species. Actually, the doctor in the play is himself a patient. Dr. Richardson, the celebrated socialist and specialist in Tuberculosis has only one spare bed in his hospital and he has to choose between an honest citizen and a rotten artist. Before making a decision, the doctor falls in love with the wife of the man of versatile genius and the introduction of the women creates complexity. The medico-economic problem is also a great bridge in the evolution of man into a superman. Truly speaking, Shaw does not skip over the real problems of poverty because it remains a degrading aspect of human life while it is likely to cause delay in the evolution of man into a better man. His revolt against the marriage system is a revolt against its sentimentality, its romance, its amorous character for the improvement of the human lot. *In Major Barbara*, he shows that Christianity can pretend to guard humanity, only because it has sold its own soul to the Devil. Society is governed by a set of men who wield the forces of vested interest. Capitalism is another major problem because it generates poverty and finally makes a hindrance in the evolution of the human race.

1. *Ibid.*, p. 86.

Shaw's *St. Joan* is a perfect specimen of historical play packed with thought-provoking ideas. Joan is a symbolic representation of creative force of the evolutionary principle and will-power. The tragedy of her life has thus a dual significance. It is the tragedy of an individual asserting for her identity and for the liberation of the human spirit from the mighty forces of law. It is at the same moment the struggle of the evolutionary principles of freedom of judgement against the Roman Catholic negation of it. Joan represents a power greater than herself:

> "I believe that God is wiser than I; and it is His commands that I will do. All the things that you call my crimes have come to me by the commands of God. I say that I have done them by the order of God; It is impossible for me to say anything else; if the Churchman says the contrary I shall not mind him: I shall mind God alone, whose command I always follow.[1]

It is the creative will of Life-Force that she obeys. Will-power can change the destiny of human life. The play is not a tragedy in the ordinary sense of the term. Joan was burnt for witchcraft but she is the expression of the Protestant idea struggling against the Roman Catholic Church, and thus a historical projection of the eternal propularian of human will and creativity towards greater freedom. Shaw suggests that the evolution of man into superman demands a conquest over passion and the perfection of the will. Napoleon in *The Man of Destiny* is an example of similar endeavour.

1. *The Complete Plays of G.B. Shaw* published in 1965, Hamlyn; London, p. 926.

IV

The Flowers and the Fruits

> Bernard Shaw wishes to show himself not so much as an optimist, but rather as a sort of faithful and wretched pessimist.[1]

Back to Methuselah provides a dismal picture of the world which is inhabited by supermen and superwomen. It reminds one of the Honyhuhumland in *Gulliver's Travels*. It appears to be incredible that Bernard Shaw had visualized a utopia in which life itself had become a burden. Men and women reached middle age at the age of four and thereafter went about thinking only of the problems of the soul, though soul they appeared to have none. When Ecrasia in Part V of *Back to Methuselah* accuses the He-Ancient and the She-Ancient of blaspheming against nature and against man, the She-Ancient tells her how life is nothing but a burden to those who know that they will not breath their last for centuries:

> Child, Child, how much enthusiasm will you have for man when you have endured eight centuries of him, as I have, and seen him perish by an empty mischance that is yet a certainty? When I discarded my dolls as he discarded his friends and his mountains, it was to myself I turned as to the final reality. Here, and here alone, I could shape and create when my arm was weak and I willed it to be strong, I could create a roll of muscle in it; and when I understood that, I understood that I could without any greater miracle give myself ten arms and three heads.[2]

---

1. G.K. Chesterton: *George Bernard Shaw*, Guild Books, London W.C.I., 1951, p. 83.
2. G.B. Shaw: *Complete Plays with Prefaces*, Vol. II, Dodd, Mead and Company, New York, 1962, p. 252.

It is inconceivable that Shaw visualized as an ideal a race of people for whom art, and the pleasures of the body, did not exist. The He-Ancient and the She-Ancient, who appear at the end of *Back to Methuselah*, are in a way Shaw's comment on the superman. These people could grow limbs at will and could destroy the lives of other persons. But the realisation came to them that such powers were not only unnecessary but also burdensome. They were fed-up with the dull, monotonous centuries which spread out before them and had lost interest in everything whatsoever. The She-Ancient informs the youngsters how she had tried to divert herself by growing extra limbs, but ultimately this struck her as childish and she was compelled, by the realisation of her folly, to give up this kind of diversion:

> ...for five more years I made myself into all sorts of fantastic monsters. I walked upon a dozen legs: I worked with twenty hands and a hundred fingers: I looked to the four quarters of the compass with eight eyes out of four heads.Children fled in amazement from me until I had to hide myself from them; and the ancients, who had forgotten how to laugh, smiled grimly when they passed.[1]

She diverted herself for quite some time, but ultimately gave up the play because she found that it was nothing if not foolish:

> One day, when I was tired of learning to walk forward with some of my feet and backwards with others and sideways with the rest all at ones, I sat on a rock with my four chins resting on four of my knees. And suddenly it came into my mind that this monstrous machinery of heads and limbs was no more me than my statues had been me, and that it was only an automation that I had enslaved.[2]

The supermen and the superwomen as they appear in *Back to Methuselah* are not only the ugliest of people imaginable, but also the most shoddily dressed. As a matter of fact, they have lost every interest in things around them including their own bodies. They believe that what really matters is the mind, and also that the mind can exist without the body. They are therefore willing to shed their head, just as the homo

1. *Ibid.*, p. 252
2. *Ibid.*, pp. 252-53.

erectus had shed his tail. As the She-Ancient informs, none of them believed that "All this machinery of flesh and blood is necessary."[1] As a matter of fact, they aim at freeing themselves completely from the tyranny of the body. The She-Ancient says at one place:

> It is this stuff (indicating her body), this flesh and blood and bone and all the rest of it, that is intolerable. Even prehistoric man dreamed of what he called an astral body, and asked who would deliver him from the body of this death.[2]

The playwright makes the ideal superpersons rather repulsive in their appearance. The He-Ancient has, on his person nothing except "a sort of linen kilt consisting mainly of girdle carrying a sporran and a few inner pockets."[3] His face "bears a net-work of lines, varying from furrows to hair-breadth reticulations."[4] He is bald without a trace of hair; as a matter of fact, he has no hair above the neck except for the eye-lashes. The She-Ancient is exactly like the He-Ancient "equally bald, and equally without sexual charm, but intensely interesting and rather terrifying. Her sex is discoverable only by her voice, as her breasts are manly, and her figure otherwise I not very different."[5] Like the He-Ancient, she also wears no clothes, though she has draped herself rather perfunctorily with a ceremonial robe. The appearance of these two superpersons on the scene dampens the mirth of the youngsters and also produces a rather bitter taste in the mouth of the readers and the spectators of the play. One wonders if Bernard Shaw was not creating a utopia of the same kind as that of the utopia of his senior compatriot Jonathan Swift. It is a bit rather absurd to believe that Swift could consider horses to be the ideal race who had the right to judge mankind. In the case of Bernard Shaw also, one is tempted to believe that the artist was creating a race of ideal people with his tongue in the cheek.

The superpersons have become fed up with the demands of the body and are nauseated with the company of human beings. They are self-contained persons who do not need the company of others and who keep aloof from others of their own kind. They are so self-centered that "they

1. *Ibid.*, p. 255.
2. *Ibid.*, p. 256.
3. *Ibid.*, p. 205.
4. *Ibid.*
5. *Ibid.*, p. 214.

have forgotten how to speak; how to read; even how to think,"[1] like others. They have acquired the power of telepathic communications. The two ancients appear on the scene whenever they are wanted, though no one tells them that they are wanted. But the power of knowing the thoughts of others, of getting everything done only by wishing it, of seeing into the past and the future, has not made them happy. They continue to remain the slaves of their bodies. They could shed their superfluous heads and hands and feet, but they could not dispense with the body altogether. They aspired for deliverance from the bondage of the body and getting metamorphosed into pure thoughts.

The elders of the world of supermen are evidently not happy nor is their fate better than that of the ordinary men and women who inhabit the world of today. Men and women of the world that we know, have many problems which keep them struggling for the whole of their lives. But they are not fed-up with their body, and their life, in the way in which the superpersons of Shaw's utopia are. The diseases, the murders, the day-to-day persecutions and a thousand other problems which keep them busy all their life along fail to make them as unhappy as the superpersons of Shaw's utopia finds themselves to be.

The elders are discontented with their lot; but what about the youngers? Born from eggs of they are, they are left to fend for themselves, since the first moment of their birth. As a matter of fact, they are children who do not know their own parents, and who do not care to know them. When a child comes out of its egg, it is already as grown up as a boy or girl of seventeen is, and the first thing that it thinks about is pleasure. It knows that it will lose the power of enjoying itself in less than four years and will then face a whole eternity of dull and monotonous existence. All that makes life worthwhile—art, literature, fancy, love—has hardly any meaning for even the young persons of this utopia. All that they can understand is the pleasure of the senses. When Aijillax tells Ecrasia that he is prepared to admire her figure only from a distance and is not ready to allow her to come near him, she haughtily leaves him because such an admiration would give her no pleasure. These people are denied even the pleasure of sleep. Somehow they have arrived at the conclusion that they must suck pleasure from every minute of the four years that they have of staying young. They are not addicted to any intoxicant but the thought

1. *Ibid.*, p. 256.

of losing the capacity for enjoyment in less than four years whips them into perpetual restlessness. The incident of the murder of Pygmalion and of the two dolls created by him, is a symbolic representation of the murder of creativeness of every kind. Pygmalion, an extraordinary artist, carved two stone figures and with the help of the new science breathed life into them. These new people, a man and a woman, were endowed with the same passions as those of ordinary men and women. They were passionate, fanciful, whimsical, self-centred and also cowardly like most people of the present day human society. Such people could not be allowed to live in this utopia because they were unable to get rid of their passions.

In order to survive in this utopia one has to be without passions, and also without any human weakness whatsoever. When the dolls have to choose between their own self and another, they chose their own self; like all ordinary men and women they value their own life more than that of any other person. But the fact that they value their life at all degrades them in the eyes of the "normal" denizens of this utopia and makes them sub-human. The fact that they are afraid of death reduces them to the level of automata. Being a man means rising above passions and above love for one's own life. The He-Ancient is angry when he finds that the youngsters of the land of supermen are clamouring for the murder of the two dolls and tells them that they should be exterminated only after it has been found out whether they possess human attributes or not:

> These things are mere automata: they cannot help shrinking from death at any cost. You see that they have no self-control, and are merely shuddering through a series of reflexes. Let us see whether we cannot put a little more life into them.[1]

He does succeed in putting more life into them, because, in the face of death, the two dolls show greater love for each other than they had shown earlier. The human "weaknesses" in their nature assert themselves and each of them is ready to exchange its own life for the life of the other. But even such a sacrifice has, for the supermen, something sub-human in it. Until man has risen wholly above the power of passions and is prepared to dispense with the body altogether and live a life of the mind, he has not attained the ideal state, the state of the superman.

1. *Ibid.*, p. 242.

The inhabitants of this utopia grow out of their passions, their love for dolls, and other weaknesses, of this kind before they are four, and thereafter pursue only one goal: how to get rid of the limitations imposed by the body and live a life only of the mind. All art is only a childish game which attracts children till the age of four. As a matter of fact the highest growth of the artistic temperament is achieved inside the egg only, and after birth there is only a gradual shrinking of this gift. The real artists, Anjillax and Martellus, were born with beards which were more than three feet long, and after their birth their beards did not grow at all; they only shrank when the two Ancients of the utopian land tell the youngsters how they themselves rose above their childish weaknesses. They are neither boasting nor condemning, they are only performing their duty as guardians. They have to bring home to the youngsters the importance of rising above the infirmities that are associated with young age. The new world has to be a place where even the young people have to have no weakness for fancy, and all artistic creations have to be spurned as an exhibition of childishness.

One of the youngsters, Ecrasia, remains unconvinced even after the long harangue of the two Ancients, and remarks:

> Without art, the crudeness of reality could make the world unbearable.[1]

She says further:

> I have found a happiness in art that real life has never given me. I am intensely in earnest about art. There is a magic and mystery in art that you know nothing of.[2]

Ecrasia's feelings are nothing but a residue of the feelings which used to sway the world once upon a time. Such feelings have a hold upon the people of the new world only so long as they are immature. Moreover, even among the immature ones, there are many that have outgrown such weaknesses is not expressing his individual opinion when he says:

> Art is not honest: that is why I never could stand much of it. It is all make-believe.[3]

1. *Ibid.*, p. 249.
2. *Ibid.*, p. 250.
3. *Ibid.*

Art is not worth straining oneself for. This view is supported by the She-Ancient who says that they have now grown out of the stage in which make-believe could have satisfied them:

> ...we who are older use neither glass mirrors nor works of art. We have a direct sense of life. When you gain that you will put aside your mirrors and statues, your toys and your dolls.[1]

But the supermen also have their problems. These problems are of a kind which cannot be appreciated by the people who have not had the good luck of being the inhabitants of the world of the supermen. Their greatest worry is that they continue to remain bound by the body which is "the last doll to be discarded."[2] The He-Ancient says:

> This is my body, my blood, my brain; but it is not me. I am the eternal life, the perpetual resurrection; but (striking his body) this structure, this organism, this make-shift, can be made by a boy in a laboratory, and is held back from dissolution only by my use of it. Worse still, it can be broken by a slip of the foot, drowned; by a cramp in the stomach, destroyed by a flash from the clouds. Sooner or later, its destruction is certain.[3]

One may very legimately doubt whether the inhabitants of this utopia are really the kind of people that Shaw wanted ordinary mortals to evolve into. As a matter of fact Shaw himself realised that these ugly creatures who had "swept a way the beasts of the garden, and made an end of the crawling things and the flying things and all of them that refused to live for ever"[4] did not deserve to be the ideal for ordinary men and women. The note of sadness, and a hope for a change, for the better at which the play ends in a kind of epilogue which the writer of *Man and Superman* could not visualise. The playwright who wrote the last scene of *Back to Methuselah* is, actually, not the man who wrote *Man and Superman*. The vision remains the same but the spirit has changed. The distance between the two plays is no less great than the distance between *The Comedy of Errors* and *The Tempest*.

When the curtain falls on the inhabitants of the utopia, Adam, Eve, Cain, the Serpent and Lilith appear on the scene. Lilith, the great mother

1. *Ibid.*
2. *Ibid.*
3. *Ibid.*
4. *Ibid.*, p. 260.

of mankind, asks if the toils and sacrifices of millions of years had been worthwhile:

> I suffered unspeakably; I tore myself asunder, I lost my life, to make of my one flesh these twain, man and woman. And this is what has come of it. What do you make of it, Adam, my son?[1]

Adam is no less sad and grieved than Lilith, but he does not find the answer to her question. He, therefore, turns to Eve and says:

> I made the earth bring forth by my labour, and the women bring forth by my love. And this is what has come of it. What do you make of it, Eve, my wife?[2]

Eve is equally grieved by what has happened. She knew love and nourished her children in her womb. But now love, the great sustainer of life, is dead, and all that remains is a life of eternity devoid of all passion, all emotion. It is now a place where children are hatched in eggs which have to be sawed in order to bring out the occupants. When, little later, she says that she is satisfied and that "All's Well" it is evidently to console herself, because those that are alive are her own children, and just as she could not condemn and curse Cain, she cannot curse and condemn those that have survived even though they have killed all that was beautiful. Actually none, except the Serpent, is happy at the turn that things have taken. He feels that the turn of events has justified him. He says:

> I am justified. For I chose wisdom and the knowledge of good and evil; and now there is no evil; and wisdom and good are one.[3]

Adam's final words of pain at what has happened is, in a way, the playwright's own comment at the picture of the "brave new world" which has been projected in the play:

> I can make nothing of it, neither head nor tail. What is it all for? Why? Whither? Whence? We were well enough in the garden. And now the fools have killed all the animals; and

1. *Ibid.*, p. 260.
2. *Ibid.*
3. *Ibid.*

> they are dissatisfied because they cannot be bothered with their bodies![1]

Lilith's long speech at the end of the play is undoubtedly the playwright's comment on the new 'civilization' and the new people that he presented in the last play of his great pentateuch. Man has succeeded in acquiring superhuman powers, but he has, in the process, lost all that made life worth living. Millions of years of bloodshed have produced what one can only be ashamed of:

> They have accepted the burden of eternal life. They have taken the agony from birth; and their life does not fail them even in the home of destruction. Their breasts are without milk: their bowals are gone: the very shapes of them are only ornaments for their children to admire and caress without understanding. If this enough; or shall I labour again? Shall I bring forth something that will sweep them away and make an end of them,..? I had patience with them for many ages: they tried we very surely. They do terrible things: they embraced death, and said that eternal life was a fable. I stood amazed at the malice and destructiveness of the things I had made... The pangs of another birth were already upon me when one man repented and lived three hundred years and I waited to the what would come of that. And So much came of it that the horrors of that time seem now but an evil dream.[2]

But she has not lost hope in the future of mankind because,

> Of Life only is there no end; and though of its million starry mansions many are empty and many still unbuilt, and though its vast domain is as yet unbearably desert, my seed shall one day fill it and master its matter to its uttermost confines.[3]

She is prepared to share the passionless monsters and continue to have faith in them because she knows that loss of faith will mean the end of the human race, and in that case the creation of the human race will have to be taken up anew. So instead of treating matter as an enemy, and enslaving it, she will have to bring about a reconciliation between matter

1. *Ibid.*
2. *Ibid.*, p. 261.
3. *Ibid.*, p. 262.

and spirit so that both become one. Mankind can be saved not by treating matter as an enemy and trying to dispense with the body altogether, but by getting reconciled to it.

What the supermen of Part V of *Back to Methuselah* have achieved is not something that Shaw considered to be ideal for mankind. It is an aberration rather than evolution. The imaginary world is in reality a world of deformed creatures and Shaw intended mankind to avoid an evolution in that direction.

V

The Shadow

In the Epistle Dedicatory to *Man and Superman* Shaw writes: "...'for art's sake' alone I would not face the toil of writing a single sentence."[1] The works of all great artists have some moral or educative value; all of them instruct in some way or the other. Art has a two-fold purpose: to give pleasure and to instruct. But the really great works of art teach us unconsciously, through the pleasure that they give us. We learn and imbibe values without being conscious of doing so. But Shaw is different. In the preface to every play he shrilly proclaims what theory he is going to propound and what lesson he is going to preach in it. He has even pretensions of being a philosopher himself. But in spite of his pretensions he has no philosophy of his own, not even a consistent system of thought to which he can stick for a fairly long time; he is a chameleon thinker who gives up and adopts ideas with apparently just one consistency: the central argument about the teleology of evolution running through his works.

Shaw has at one place declared that "he was a free thinker before he knew how to think." This is certainly right. He inherited this trait from his father who was a lewd cynic, and who, after having taught the Bible to his son when the latter was small, for an hour or two, would hurl the book across the room exclaiming, "It's all a pack of damned lies." This cynicism remained an inseparable part of Shaw's character throughout his whole life. He remained vacillating in his convictions, shifting from one system to another, and sometimes believing in opposite systems of thought at the same time.

His family background made him an atheist when he was in his teens: "...my development was in a family atmosphere so skeptical, Bohemian,

1. G.B. Shaw: *Man and Superman*, Penguin Books, Harmondsworth-Middlesex, 1951, p. xxxvii.

anarchic, and on its educational side aesthetic, that in my teens I was a professed atheist..." The realisation that God did not exist dawned on him suddenly: "I suddenly asked myself why I went on repeating my prayer every night, when, as I put it, I did not believe in it." And he did a revolutionary thing; he did not say his prayers that night!

In 1876, at the age of twenty, he came to London with his mother, and in 1882 he happened to listen to a lecture on land nationalisation delivered by Henry George. The result was like a revelation "It flashed on me that the conflict between religion and science... the overthrow of the Bible, the higher education of women, Mill on Liberty and all the rest of the storm that raged around Darwin, Tyndall, Huxley, Spencer and the rest, on which I had brought myself up intellectually, was a mere middle class business ...The importance of the economic basis dawned on me." He read Henry George's *Progress and Poverty*. Then some one told him to read *Das Capital*. The result was that "Karl Marx made a man of me."

The economic depression of the eighteen eighties had caused a new storm of socialist agitation. Bernard Shaw could not but be influenced by the new fashion and he became a socialist. He spoke in halls, on street corners, in Hyde Park, in order to bring about socialism in a few hours. But after the *Bloody Sunday* of November 1887, when the workers were brutally massacred by the police, the agitation quieted down, and the socialist enthusiasm of Bernard Shaw also vanished.

At one place in Epistle Dedicatory to *Man and Superman* he writes, "...there is no future for men, however brimming with crude vitality, who are neither intelligent nor politically educated enough to be socialists."[1] But, in spite of his lip service to socialism, except for a limited period during the eighties and the nineties of the last century—when he wrote his only socialist plays *The Widowers' Houses* and *Mrs. Warren's Profession* —, he has never really been a practising socialist. His political writings are uncertain in their attitude, and when after long, tedious, and pointless arguments he has finished, he leads us nowhere; we remain where we were when we began. He shouts and fumes, but there is really no inner fire and, as he himself once acknowledged, no idea to hurt any body, not even the capitalists, whose enemy, as a socialist, he professes to be. He is not able to mobilise against capitalism the kind of intense resentment which Voltaire trained on the Church. As a matter of fact he has never been the single-minded crusader he was at times I supposed to be.

1. *Ibid.*, p. xviii.

The socialist agitation of the eighties having quieted down, Shaw became "sober". He attached himself to the statistical Sydney Webb, and they, with some others, founded the Fabian Society which "agreed to give up the delightful case of the revolutionary heroics and take to the hard work of practical reform on ordinary parliamentary lines." Shaw became a vestryman and then a borough councillor. The Fabians continued to treat Marx with respect but they discredited some of his main assumptions and "revised" Marxism. They shifted the value of commodities produced from the labourer to the consumer. They repudiated the class-war and asserted that it would never occur. Socialist nationalisation was to be accomplished by a corpus of experts who should "permeate" government and business, quietly invading Whitehall and setting up detachments which, unassisted by the action of the masses, should put socialist ideas into effect. The Fabians, as a matter of fact, vulgarised Marxism made it devoid of all its revolutionary essence, and transformed it into a cheap bourgeois slogan to deceive the masses. And then Shaw boasted that the Fabians had made socialism respectable!

But he could not, for a long time, believe in "practical reform on ordinary parliamentary lines." By 1903, his socialism had modified itself to such an extent that he could no longer believe in the wisdom of the masses. In the Epistle Dedicatory to *Man and Superman* he says,

> "What our voters are in the pit and gallery, they are also in the polling booth. We are all now under what Burke called the hoofs of the swinish multitude. Give these people the most perfect political constitution and the soundest political programme that benevolent omniscience can devise for them, and they will interpret it into mere fashionable folly or canting charity as a savage converts the philosophical theology of a Scotch missionary into crude African idolatry."[1]

So the masses, the common people, had not brains enough to see the perfectness of the political constitution and the soundness of the political programme that Shaw was prepared, in his generosity of heart, to bestow upon them.

> "Hence we must either breed political capacity or be ruined by democracy, which was forced on us by the failure of the

1. *Ibid.*, p. xxiv.

> older alternatives. Yet, if despotism failed only for want of a capable benevolent despot, what chance has democracy, which requires a whole population of capable voters..."[1]

The conclusion is: The future is dark, because the problem of breeding "political capacity" is a really difficult one.

But there is no reason to be disheartened about the future. Shaw cannot only discover problems, he can also offer solutions. Here is the solution: "The overthrow of the aristocrate has created the necessity of the Superman."[2] *The Revolutionist's Handbook* was intended to be *The Communist Manfesto* of the new revolution which Shaw was going to bring about. In the *Handbook*, he has propounded a complete revolutionary theory, and has tried to say things that are startling and revolting. Whatever might have been the reaction of the readers when it was first published, today it reads like an empty intellectual exercise. How to avoid the political catastrophe of the past?

> "To that recurrent catastrophe we shall certainly come again unless we have a Democracy of Supermen; and the production of such a Democracy is the only change that is now hopeful enough to nerve us to the effort that Revolution demands."[3]

And the democracy of supermen can be produced only if supermen are produced first, which is possible only through 'eugenics' selective breeding. They can be produced only promiscuously because, "marriage when it is made an indispensable condition of meeting' will delay the advent of the Superman effectually."

Shaw did not stick long to the absurd idea of selective breeding and the creation of the superman, and sauntered off, with his characteristic ease, to other panaceas for the solution of the problems that face human beings. But in *Back to Methuselah* (1921), he gave a picture of his democracy of supermen. In this play, he visualises a human society in which four years after birth every one reaches the physical and emotional detachment of old age, and all the glamour which sex, animal spirits, the delight of the senses, land to experience, vanishes. The Ancients, in the last part of *Back to Methuselah*, having achieved a relative emancipation from the needs and exigencies of matenal existence, employ their freedom

1. *Ibid.*, p. xxvi.
2. *Ibid.*
3. *Ibid.*, p. 244.

in the unfettered activity of the intellect. They have achieved complete mastery over their bodies, can create surplus arms and legs at will, have power over others also and can apparently kill with a glance. It is in the creation of such creatures that Shaw sees the salvation of humanity.

In the meantime Shaw's ideas had undergone another change, and by 1905 he saw the end of human suffering in the mutual doing away with all vestiges of the class struggle, in a permanent reconciliation between the exploiters and the exploited. *In Major Barbara* (1905) he advanced the idea of alliance between the worker and the capitalist as the sole remedy of all social evils. His socialism and Fabianism were gone with the wind. Like his hero, Anrew Undershaft, he had come to know what it was to make one's way in capitalist society, and to occupy a position of power. He had become the type of the critic who, by scolding the bourgeoisie, makes good with it and becomes one of its idols. He was gradually, for all the scandal associated with his early life, turning into one of the most solid and sensible members of the British propertied classes. How could he ally himself with the poor masses now? How could he sacrifice money, prestige and power for the swinish multitude?

But he did not stop at the idea of alliance between the workers and the capitalists; he really became a full-blooded imperialist in courses of time. Though he was an Irishman, in *John Bull's Other Island* (1914), he backed English imperialism against the Irish freedom movement on account of what he considered to be the superior enterprise and pragmatism of the English. He supported the English against the Boers at the time of the South African war because the Boers represented for him a backward civilisation. This was nothing less than supporting the idea of racial superiority, which in later years became the basis of new ideologies and governments. When the First World War began, he wrote *Commonsense about the War*, which is a double-faced document. He talks of socialism democracy, religion, God, civilisation, and everything; and after a long and spirited bombast the conclusion he arrives at is that the War must be supported and vigorously prosecuted. Shaw must support England, his "ward", in her "distress", because "as I had practically adopted England by thrusting myself and my opinions on her in the face of every possible rebuff, it was for me to take the consequences which certainly included an obligation to help my reluctant ward in her extremity as far as my means allowed." When all the genuine socialists of the world were denouncing the war, Bernard Shaw, the respectable socialist, supported the English imperialists.

But Shaw, the constant seeker after truth, again found out new ways for the salvation of humanity—ways not only different from those discovered by him in the past, but in certain cases quite opposed to them. In 1916, he published a volume of plays containing *Androcles and the Lion, Overruled and Pygmalion*, and a long preface on Christianity and its founder. In it he wrote:

> "After contemplating the world and human nature for nearly sixty years, I see no way out of the world misery but the way which would have been found by Christ's will if he had undertaken the work of a modern practical statesman."

Shaw now concluded that the end of human misery lay not in socialism nor in the creation of the superman, but in Christianity as Shaw would have developed it into. In another play, *Saint Joan* (1924), he idealised religious inspiration.

Shaw had got the unusual talent of effecting compromise between directly opposite systems of thought, He could speak both for socialism and religion in the same breath. He could be a socialist propagandist and an advocate of hero-worship simultaneously. In *Man of Destiny* (1907), *Caesar and Cleopatra* (1913), *Augustus Does His Best* (1917) and some other plays he exalted the idea of hero-worship. This exaltation of the individual and minimisation of the role of the masses persisted throughout his career. A typical bourgeoisie intellectual that he was, he could not see the other side of the coin. His narrow individualism prevented him from looking at these historical personalities objectively; all of them, be he Napoleon, Caesar, Augustus and Christ are Shaw himself put in their respective positions.

In his political utterances since the First World War, Shaw created a scandal by taking absurd positions on important issues. In 1927, he went to Fascist Italy, and the excellence of the Fascist system dawned on him. He became a staunch supporter and admirer of Mussoloni. Mussoloni had, according to Shaw, "achieved a dictatorship in a great modern state without a single advantage, social, official or academic, to assist him, after marching to Rome with a force of Black Shirts with a single disciplined regiment." And when some one pointed out to him the fallacy of this contention, he exclaimed with a characteristic tragic gesture, "Oh, I shall die soon!"

After his visit to the Soviet Union in 1931, he praised the Soviet system for a time and scolded the U.S.A. for not following the Soviet example. Later, in his *Preface on Bosses* in his volume of plays published in 1936, he was back praising Mussoloni again and even throwing a few kind words for Hitler. He described Hitler's persecution of the Jews as a loophole in his statesmanship. Of the systematic persecution by the Nazis of Socialists, Communists, and Paficists, of every body, including critics and artists, who belonged to Shaw's own camp, he had nothing to say except to mention it and minimise it in passing as "plundering raids and 'coup de etat' against inconvenient Liberals and Marxists." At the time of the Ethiopian War. he came out strongly for Mussoloni on the same ground on which he had formerly defended the behaviour of the British in South Africa. He insisted that the League of Nations should never have tried to interfere.

In *The Apple Cart* (1929), a very topical play, he pleaded for strong monarchy as the only remedy for all political evils. Kind Magnus is presented as far superior to his cabinet ministers in political understanding and disinterestedness. The central idea that emerges from the criscross of discussions from the satire, from the fun and the characters is that democracy as a form of government is a hopeless fraud, and that the real remedy lies in strong monarchy.

The vacillating element in Shaw's character was not something accidental. His father belonged to a family of ruined nobility, and his mother also, who was expected to marry at least a duke, was from a similar family. When Shaw, in the beginning of his career, found himself no better than an ordinary labourer, his "noble" blood revolted against the whole social system. But his revolt was only a camouflage to serve his own personal interests. His bourgeois individualism prevented him from feeling any real sympathy for the masses, and he was disgusted with them. So he vacillated from one view to another until he gained fame and power when he began to support the capitalist class more or less consistently. But because of the peculiar insecure position of the bourgeois intellectual in capitalist society, and because of his early socialist indoctrinisation, he could really never feel himself to be one with the capitalist class. So he always vacillated, and could find conviction nowhere.

George Bernard Shaw was a thinker, but in essentials his ideas do not differ from those of other thinkers who had already written on the subjects on which Shaw wrote at a later stage. But even this would not have mattered much had he stuck to one philosophy of life instead of changing his ideas, and made all his plays, or at least the majority of them a medium for the expression of that philosophy. But instead of sticking to one philosophy, he changed it like his coat, with the result that he sometimes contradicted himself. Although the idea of superman could be mistaken as one of the many ideas he played with, the fact is that it has roots in the only consistent and fairly continuous principle behind all his thought: the principle of Life-Force and evolution related to biology and spirit—values more enduring than socialism or politics or war.

Shaw's significance as a thinker lies not in making quantitative adjustment and balancing of various incongruous elements and methods of production but in suggesting a qualitative change over to something different and new, from which various social consequences flow. The economic, and political aspects of this qualitative change are important but equally so are the social and psychological aspects. He desired to change the static character of our living and to make it dynamic and vital in order to release man into a greater awareness of life's purpose. The diversity of his ideas is obvious but this belongs to the surface.

He propounds the concept of superman to meet the challenge of the contemporary problems of the human life by readjusting the basic orientation of existence. Napoleon in *The Man of Destiny* has ingredients of a casual superman but still he lacks the quality of a Methuselah. Shaw is not a rebel like P.B. Shelly and Ibsen but on the other hand he is a champion of socialism and evolutionary process who pleads strongly for waging a war against social injustice and social disparity, questioning the ethics of heroism in the context of the greater courage to survive:

> "I brave! How little you know! I have spent the day in agony of fear. I have a pain here from the tightening of my heart as every suspicious look, every threatening movement. Do you think every one is as brave as you? Oh, why will not you brave people—do the brave things? Why do you leave them to us, who have no courage at all? I am not brave: I shrink from violence: danger makes me miserable.[1]

The conventional value of courage and violence hampers the grow th of human sensibility and brings disharmony and annihilation to the

1. *Ibid.*, p. 160.

human race. He does not support war in *Arms and the Man* because the solution of the problems, or human life does not live in war. It creates a problem and it is a serious huddle in the evolution of creative genius. Purification of the soul demands complete sacrifice for the development of the human race. Napoleon in *The Man of Destiny* says:

> Self-sacrifice is the foundation of all true nobility of character.[1]

The hall-mark of supermen and superwomen should be self-sacrifice, love and pity. The basic requirement for change is the quality of love. Change through love is creative and will bring a kind of newness in one s attitude to contemporary problems.

> Do you think that If I wanted those dispatches only for myself, I dare venture into a battle for them? No: If that were all, I should not have the courage to ask to see at your Hotel, even my courage is mere slavishness: It is of no use to me for my own purposes. It is only through love, through pity, through the instinct to save and to protect someone else, that I can do the things that terrify me."[2]

These define the preserving, motherly care for life, taking away the film of romance from heroism and romance. In *Arms and the Man* Raina is still a woman torn between reality and romance. Bluntschli is a brilliant predecessor to superman like Napoleon of *The Man of Destiny*. His early supermen and superwomen figuring in early plays do not have the identity with Life-Force so much as an intellectual awareness of it. Intellect itself is an effective antidote to romance. In *Candida* Shaw exposes the idea of romance springing from withdrawal, egotism and fantasy. Marchbanks says:

> (Stopping her mysteriously) Hush! I go about in search of love: And I find it in the measured stores in the bosoms of others. But when I try to ask for it, this horrible shyness strangles me and I stand dumb or worse than dumb saying meaningless things foolishly. And I see the affection I am longing for given to dogs and cats and pet birds, because they come and ask for

1. *Ibid.*, p. 170.
2. *Ibid.*, p. 161.

> it (almost whispering). It must be asked for: It is like a ghost: It cannot speak unless it is first spoken to ... All the love the world is longing to speak; only it dare not, because it is shy! shy! shy! that is world's tragedy.[1]

Shyness is here recoil from life which is cured by his being exposed to the ruthless and instinctive courage and wisdom of Candida. She derives there from here identity with Life-Force as a woman—responsible for propagation of the race. The main pursuit of woman is the pursuit of evolution of man into superman.

In St. Joan, the identity of woman widi the large forces is embodied in her trust and instinct and will.

The impact of Bergson helped Shaw to sort out his basic ideas as in *Back to Methuselah*. Bergson's philosophy, unlike most of the systems of the past, is dualistic. The world, for him, is divided into two separate parts: on the one hand life, on the other hand intellect. The whole universe is the clash and conflict of two opposite motions: Life which climbs upward and matter which pulls downward. Evolution of man into superman is not primarily explicable by adaptation to environment; adaptation explains only the turns and twists of evolution like windings of a road approaching a town dirough hilly country. Bergson provides for Shaw the belief that evolution is truly creative, like the work of an artist. Evolution is unpredictable and capable of changes brought about by will rather than environment. Life-Force is an indispensable factor for evolution because it pushes us on from behind restlessly and unceasingly. But Life-Force operates in a complex war. *Arms and the Man* does not only reveal Life-Force operating through Raina and Bluntschli, it also highlights the inevitable barrier of romance in love which blocks evolution. Had Raina surrendered to Sergius the play would have become a fine example of a romance. Shaw's emphasis is on 'selection' between sexes because this is more fundamental to evolution. Bluntschli, like Tanner, is in the grip of Life-Force. Bluntschli says in *Arms and the Man*:

No, my dear young lady, no, no, no a thousand times. Its part of your youth: Part of your charm, I am like all the rest of them: the nurse, your parents, Sergius: Im your infatuated admirer.[2]

---

1. *Ibid.*, p. 135.
2. *Ibid.*, p. 58.

Shaw clarifies that when Life-Force possess a man, he becomes a passive victim to female charm. Shaw has counterpointed the themes of love and war because he believed that war is a waste of mans resources while love is desirable and conducive to the biological purpose of human existence. Shaws humorous use of love and marriage has both the seriousness of its implied purpose and of Shaws own experience. As A.C. Ward writes:

> In Arms and the Man and often elsewhere he laughed at this and other solemnities, but behind the humour of relationship of Raina, Sergius and Bluntschli lay the memories of Shaws own childhood in a home shadowed by the failure of his own parents marriage.[1]

Darwin made a deep effect on Shaw. Darwins doctrine of evolution is not a new one but an old one propounded by Lamarck and Darwins grand father Erasmus. Darwins theory has two parts, on one hand is the theory of evolution which maintains the different aspects of life have developed from a common ancestory. The second part of his theory is the struggle for existence and the survival of the fittest. What is interesting from the historical point of view is Darwins extension to the whole of life of the economics that characterised the philosophical radicals. The motive force of evolution in the opinion of Darwin is a form of biological economics in a world of free competition. Darwin himself was very liberal, but his doctrines had many repercussions in some ratio to conventional liberalism.

Darwins idea of the survival of the fittest as a pattern of evolution gave an unsuspected strength to Nietzsches notion of superman who rose to his full stature through bitter competition.

> I teach you the Superman. Man is something that should be overcome.
>
> *** *** ***
>
> Man is rope, fastered between animal and superman—a rope over an abbey.[2]
>
> (*Thus Spoke Zarathustra*)

1. Shaw: *Arms and the Man,* Macmillan, 1965, p. 98.
2. *Hollingdale: A Nietzsche Reader,* p. 237, Penguin books, 1977.

Shaws rejection of popular certainties and values in his belief in superman has Nietzsches belief in superiority:

> Overcome, you higher man, the pitty virtues, the petty produces, the sand-grain discretion, the ant-swarm inanity, miserable eerie, the happiness of the greatest number.[1]

Nietzsches hero or great man ranges from the mythical Zarathustra to his shadow projected on European history which Carlyle aggrandizes and whose deformed spectre turned out to be Adolf Hitler.

Tolstoys War and Peace is an attempt to identify the superman and to exercise the ghost but a vain one, for the spectre has never been so powerful as at the present. Shaws treatment of Caesar in *Caesar and Cleopatra* is not so much a mockery of the superman as of the historical great man who is revealed to be small in comparison to the womanhood of Cleopatra. Caesar stands for war and conquest which are belifted not in contrast to Cleopatras ageless charm of a romantic kind but to the ageless woman and her function in the scheme of Life-Force that she is.

What is preferred in glorified history comes under similar observation in *The Applicant*, where Shaw works out the story of conflict between England and her labour cabinet in order to expose the hollowness of the cabinet which promotes exploitation and creates a hindrance in the evolution of the human race. Shaw criticises the present system of democracy and exposes the hollowness of the government headed by ministers who work under the guidance of powerful personality and waste major portion of their challenge and time in bungling and exploitation. Much of what Shaw had to say of the evils of the democracy he puts into the mouth of the king Magnus who holds that democracy is not ruled by public and that elected rulers dupe the common people.

Election as a method of democracy is not simply the root cause of all evils but also a great hurdle in the efflorescnce of the humanity. Democratic election as a means of selecting qualified rulers is merely a trick and an illusion to dupe the poor. Shaw clearly shows that the cabinet is a collection of noodless and windbags who instead of doing their duty spoil their time in arguing.

Shaw attacks democracy in *Heart Break House* which he began writing in a mood of desperation in the year 1913. This play reflects the picture of sophisticated, cultured, leisured Europe before the First

---

1. *Ibid.*, p. 243.

World War. Shaw warns that the misuse of the political institutions will cause disaster in the evolution of the human race. *Heart Break House* is an embodiment of heart-breaking inefficiency of capitalist democracy which causes stagnation in the progress of the human race. Captain Shotover, standing on the improvised bridge in a gale has grown too old now to keep his memory fresh. Providence always takes the drunken skippers on the rocks, though every drunkard trusts providence. Yet, under the eccentric exterior of captain Shotover can be glimpsed a foretaste of isolation, detachment, and faith in a purpose greater than political ideals—the virtues of the Superman.

Democracy today is the rule of spoilers and oppressors. The evolution of the human race demands a government of skilled people to run the government. Shaw accepts the role of education and he considers education as a vehicle of improving the intellectual efficiency of man. His recipe is eugenics. Able rulers must be bred and thus he crosses over from politics to biology. A believer in the race of superman, Shaw had a great faith in individuals talent. Shaws bias against democracy is partly due to his experience of the inaptitude of democracy and partly in the creation of the superman. It follows that so long as we have a superman among us, we should follow him blindly. Sergius and Petkoff should be controlled by Bluntschli. But what is to be done when there is no hope for superman? Shaw was a free thinker as soon as he learnt to think. But what about the thinking of Russia? Shaw smiles at the idea of justice in the capitalistic society. Genuine democracy can help to a great extent in the evolution of man into superman. He exposes the hollowness of democracy as it is found in actual practice.

In the preface to *Getting Married*, Shaw asserts that the notion that Democracy means governing the country according to the ignorance of majority is disastrously wrong and damaging for the evolution of the Man. Evidently enough, Shaw desires democracy but not ready to acknowledge the framed view of Abraham Lincoln that Democracy is a government of the people, for the people and by the people. The postulate of Shavian evolution and state is a democratic franchise. Here, there are two cabinet of administrators. The Shavian state and Shavian evolution are thus in touch with the people and they must satisfy the requisite demand of the people in order to provide a blueprint for the growth of human race. Truly speaking, Shaws idea of superman is to some extent similar to that of Plato. Thinking is not an addition to human knowledge but also an improvement upon human growth.

A clear point in Shaws drama is the dialectical pattern comprehending (1) a rigorous insistence on values implied by Life-Force and the idea of the superman, and (2) an equally determined application of these values to the distortions and aberrations of social, political, and economic situations. Only superficially can this be regarded as an example of satire; moreover, Shaws values has to be the general sanction which has to be the base of a satire. More specifically, this dialectics seems to stand for Shaws concern for both values, and effective drama; the latter depends largely on the sense of actual people and situations without which it would be reduced, to stock emblems and purification. What is not quite as obvious, however, is that this dialectics is a specific Shavian expression of a characteristically contemporary concern showed by almost all major writers in the first quarter of this century. Stripped of its specific aspects, it is an expression for the general feeling of disparity and scheme between the fundamental and the superficial, minority culture and mass civilization, order and anarchy which finds varieties of expression in the works of Forster, Yeats, Eliot, Joyce and Lawrence. Shaws sense of order, purpose and centrality is embodied in his ideas of Life-Force creative evolution and superman which project human existence and its meaning upon the backdrop of cosmic-biological timelessness. This has its analogy with the idea of meaningful culture in Forster, and with the dialectics posed by Yeats, Eliot, Joyce and Lawrence between the timeness and universal order of myth and the panorama of futility and anarchy which is contemporary history.[1] In terms of analogy more than similarity, the clarity and finality of Shaws reorientation of social, political and economic to the basic problems of the race, is comparable to the definition of contemporary experience in Yeats, Eliot and Joyce within the meaningful framework of myth. A lost of contemporary problems find not only their answer in Shaws analogous idea of the superman but gain a proper context, shape and significance. The idea of evolution and superman functions like a myth when , approximated to and interfused with the issues of a women in family (Candida), Mostrtution (Mrs. Warren), inspiration and authority (Joan), democracy and the minority elite (Heart Break House), war, romance, heroism, etc. Lilith in *Back to Methuselah* is the mythical mother of mankind, the very womb of life, who stands for the inclusive presence of Shaws myth and the way it informs the minutest details of existence-shaping them even when they appear to be most out of shape as in contemporary life.

1. *T.S. Eliot:* –, Order and Myth (Dial 1923, p. 480-83).

Select Bibliography

Works by Bernard Shaw

Standard Edition of the Works of Bernard Shaw (Constable and Company Ltd., London).

Advice to a Young Critic, Letters 1894-1928, (Peter Owen Ltd., London).

Ellen Terry and Bernard Shaw: A Correspondence, Edited by St. John Christopher (Constable & Co. Ltd., London, 1931).

What I Really Wrote about the War (Constable & Co., London, 1931).

Shaw on Theatre, Edited by E.J. West (Hill and Wang, New York, 1958).

Shaw on Shakespeare, Edited and with an Introduction by Edwin Wilson (Cassell, London, 1962).

Bernard Shaw, W.B. Yeats, Letters to Florence Farr. Edited by Clifford Bax (Home & Van Thal Ltd., London, 1946).

The Matter with Ireland, Edited with an Introduction, by David H. Greene and Dan H. Laurence (Rupert Hart-Davis, Soho Square, London, 1962).

Books on Bernard Shaw

Bentley, Eric, *Bernard Shaw* (Robert Bale Ltd., London, 1950).

Chestorton, G.K., *George Bernard Shaw* (The Bodley Head, London, 1950).

Colboume, Maurice, *The Real Bernard Shaw* (J.M. Dent Sons Ltd., London, 1949).

Duffin, Henry Charles, *The Quintessence of Bernard Shaw* (Allen & Unwn Ltd., 1920).

Ervine, St. John, *Bernard Shaw: His life, Works and Friends* (Constable & Company Ltd., 1956).

Harris, Frank, *Bernard Shaw: Playboy and Prophet* (Victor Gollancz Ltd., London, 1931).

Henderson, Archibald, *Bernard Shaw* (D. Appleton & Company, New York, 1932).

——, *George Bernard Shaw: The Man of the Century* (Appleton Century Crofts Inc., New york, 1956).

Joad, C.E.M., *Shaw* (Victor Gollancz Ltd., London, 1949).

——, *Shaw and Society: An Anthology and A Symposium* (Odhams Press Ltd., London).

MacCarthy, Desmond, *Shaw* (Macgibbon & Kee, London, 1951).

Nethercot, Arthus H., *Men and Supermen, The Shavian Portrait Gallery* (Harvard University Press Cambridge, 1954).

Patch, Balanche, *Thirty Years with G.B.S.* (Victor Gollancz Ltd., London, 1951).

Pearson, Hesketh, *A Full Length Portrait* (Garden City Publishing Co. Inc., New York, 1946).

——, G.B.S.: *A Postscript* (Collins, London, 1951).

Robertson, J.M., *Mr. Shaw and the Maid* (Richard Cobden-Sanderson, London).

Roy, R.N., *Bernard Shaw's Philosophy of Life* (Firma K.L. Mukhopadhyay, Culcutta, 1964).

Sen Gupta, S.C., *The Art of Bernard Shaw* (A. Mukherjee & Co., Ltd. Calcutta,, 1950).

Strauss, E., *George Bernard Shaw* (Longmans Green & Co. Ltd., London, 1950).

Ward, A.C., *Bernard Shaw* (Longmans, Green & Co., London, 1951).

West, Alick, *A Good Man Fallen Among Fabians* (Lawrence & Wishart Ltd., London, 1949).

Winsten S. (Ed.), *G.B.S. 90* (Hutchinson & Co. Ltd., London, 1946).

——, *Days with Bernard Shaw* (Hutchinson & Co. Ltd., London).

Books on Biology

Barnett, S.A., (Ed), *A Century of Darwin* (Heinemann, London, 1959).

Bergson, Henri, *Creative Evolution*, Translated by Arthur Mitchell (The Modern Library, New York, 1944).

——, *Matter and Memory*, Translated by Nacy Margaret Paul and Walter Scott Palmer (George Allen & Unwin Ltd., London, 1919).

——, *Time and Free Will*, Translated by F.L. Pogson. (George Allen & Unwin Ltd., London, 1950).

Butler, Samuel, *Evolution-Old and New*, Ed. by R.A. Stratfield. (A.C. Fifield, London, 1911).

——, *Life and Habit*, 2nd Ec. (Trubner & Com., London, 1887).

——, *Unconscious Memory*, New Ed. (A.C. Fifield, 1910).

Darwin, Charles, *The Origin of Species*, Sixth Ed. (Oxford University Press, London, 1951).

Hardy, A.C. and Ford, E.B., (Ed.), *Evolution as a Process* (George Allen & Unwin Ltd., London, 1954).

Huxley, Julian, *Evolution in Action* (A Mentor Book, The New American Library, 1953).

Huxley, Thomas Henry and Huxley, Julian, *Evolution and Ethics*, 1893-1943 (The Pilot Press Ltd., London, 1947).

Keith, Sir Arthur, *Essays on Human Evolution* (Watts & Co. London, 1914).

Lamarck, Jean Baptists, *Zoological Philosophy*, Translated by Hugh Elliot (Macmillan & Co., Ltd., London, 1914).

Shull, A. Franklin, *Evolution* (McGraw Hill Book Co., Inc. New York, 1951).

Simpson, George Gaylord, *The Meaning of Evolution* (A. Mentor Book, The New American Library, 1948).

Wells, H.G., Huxley, Julian & Wells, G.P., *The Science of Life* (Cassell & Co. Ltd., London, 1931).

Miscellaneous Books

Bradbook, M.C., *Ibsen the Norwegian* (Chatto & Windus, London, 1948).

Collins, A.S., *English Literature of the Twentieth Century* (University Tutorial Press Ltd., London, 1951).

Daiches, David, *A Critical History of English Literature*, 2 vols., (Secker & Warburg, London, 1960).

Hollingdal, *A Nietzsche Reader* (Penguin Books, Harmondsrooth, 1977).

Ibsen, Henrik, *Eleven Plays of Henrik Ibsen* (The Modern Library, New York).

Marx, Karl, *Das Kapital*, 2 Vols.

Plato, *The Republic*, Translated by Benjamin Jowett (The World Publishing Co., Cleveland and New York, 1946).

Wells, H.G., *The Outline of History* (Cassell & Co. Ltd., 1956).